Organization Design

Organization Design

An analytical approach to the
structuring of organizations

Derek Newman

Edward Arnold

© A. D. NEWMAN 1973

First published 1973
by Edward Arnold (Publishers) Ltd.
25 Hill Street
London W1X 8LL

ISBN: 0 7131 3292 2

6908

Printed in Great Britain by
T. & A. Constable Ltd., Edinburgh

Preface and Explanation of Aim

In the course of my work as a consultant and teacher with client organizations, often in depth over a long period of time, I have become convinced of two things. One is that many of the problems met in them are organizational in their origin, even if they manifest themselves in a personal or behavioural way; therefore if they are to be dealt with effectively a continuing interest in development of the organization is essential. The notion that we can get the organization right and then get on with some work is wrong, and dangerous, for organization is a process, not just a situation, and a process that evolves or degenerates through time, often in a highly dynamic way.

The second thing is that in many situations it is becoming apparent that we are approaching the end of the possibility of improving effectiveness by making further detailed improvements in existing organizations or in the techniques used in them—the next stage of development must be one of organizational design initiative and innovation. I have seen too many industrial companies, and too many institutions of other kinds, struggling to deal with problems by applying powerful and sophisticated techniques and yet failing to improve effectiveness, sometimes even reducing it, and often damaging the credibility of the technique in the process, because they have not been aware of underlying organizational features or problems, or have not been able to deal with the pressures towards different organizational forms that have been exposed by techniques, and which cannot be dealt with at the level of technique. In reality, too many people do their work in spite of the organization rather than as assisted or enabled by it. Furthermore, I think that the stage has been reached in some situations where the organization will have to be changed, away from what is desirable in purely organizational terms, in order to enable real human managers, with their fallibilities, their limitations, to be relatively competent, relatively effective in their work.

All this means that organization design is an increasingly topical subject. This book is not a comprehensive thesis of design, but a practical one, based on experience and observation in different kinds of organization, in various fields, and the approach it indicates has been used very successfully in many cases. This can be used or taught with confidence, because it enables effective decisions about design to be made; it does not itself make them. It will not tell you what the design of an organization must be for particular circumstances, since the final decisions must be made and modified in the light of all the factors in those circumstances, and some of those factors, such as that of the particular personalities involved, can only be dealt with on the spot. But it does indicate what factors must be considered, and how they interact; it gives a framework for design. It also attempts to show how to deal with those aspects of organization that cannot be designed or predicted, but whose presence must be recognized. It will not tell you what changes are needed in a specific organization; organizations are too complex for that. But it does show a methodology of design, a way of recognizing and thinking about those features whose presence is inevitable because they are basic to all organization. It sets out the main issues that I find come up over and over again in questions of organization design. Some may seem naïve, but these are the ones that often cause the most difficulty—perhaps because they are too obvious. The approach is analytical and conceptual, as any practical approach must be if it is to be more than anecdotal, and this enables the new ideas that are beginning to appear and must be developed further, and their limitations, to be assessed and fully understood. It is also a fairly elementary one, because I believe we are all really at an elementary stage of knowledge in the subject. Of course, there are plenty of apparently sophisticated views about, but too many of them are based on generalizations that have not been fully tested, or, in their sophistication, fail to recognize more primitive and perhaps rather brutal facts of organization and human behaviour.

A word of warning may be appropriate here. One experience I often have is that of seeing people in an organization, encouraged to become more sensitive to themselves and to others and to understand organizational factors and properties more clearly, becoming more demanding in their expectations of openness, honesty and objectivity in their seniors. This is a tremendously valuable feature in an organization, in terms of its effectiveness and evolution, but only if it is responded to adequately; without response it is likely to become inverted and regressive, and end in a bad rather than a good result.

The book is in two parts. In the first, basic features of organization are identified and clarified and their design implications discussed. In the second, the concepts and terminology from the first part are used in looking at broader questions of organization design. The first part describes what exists in all real organizations, to give the determinants and constraints of design. The second part explores the design options that appear to be available.

A great deal of literature on the theory of organization and its history is available; I have tried to communicate an understanding of the main features of organization design in a way that allows such theoretical or deeper and more detailed material to be linked in.

Acknowledgements

This book owes a considerable debt to the Glacier Project of research, into one particular industrial organization, and to the opportunities I had in the Glacier Institute of discussing the findings in that Project with a variety of people. This, however, produced in me a strong view that the Glacier work was not a totality but a starting point, on a fairly narrow base, and could not adequately be generalized without considerable widening of that base.

My main acknowledgement here therefore is to all those, from different fields of organization and various countries and cultures, who over the past few years have joined in the work of the Centre for Organization Analysis, criticizing, constructing, developing and refining the analytical approach and the understanding of organization that follows its use, on a base that is represented by the breadth of their combined experience, observations and data.

My third debt is to all those who assisted in the preparation of this book itself and dealt with the problems that arose in its course.

The inadequacies are my own.

DEREK NEWMAN
Fulmer,
January 1973.

Contents

Introduction

Organization design is the design of the structure of the organization, using the term structure in its widest sense, and a main theme of this book is that the way in which we think about organization structure is often too narrow. Organization design is more than the design of the pattern of positions and functions often described as the 'organization structure'; it is also the design of the organizational processes of work, in particular the decision-process, whose features are as structural in their implications as those more usually recognized in the organizational chart. These two kinds of structure interact in practice, and in order to be able to describe them I will use different expressions for each of them. The structure of positions and functions will be referred to here as the *situational structure*, and the structure of the processes as the *process structure*.

An analogy may be helpful, though, as always, it should not be taken too far. If one wishes to understand the workings of an internal combustion engine, one must examine it mechanically—this gives information about how its parts link together and interact in motion. This is the equivalent of what I have called the situational structure. One must also examine it thermodynamically—this gives information about the working fluid, how it operates, what the working cycle is. This is the equivalent of the process structure. The mechanics and the thermodynamics interact; the mechanical structure is the framework within which and through which the power process operates. The power process is the source of action and the mechanical structure achieves stability, co-ordination and control. Both structures are dynamic, but their dynamics though inter-related are not identical.

I do not think it possible to say exactly how organizations should be designed, and what activities should go on in them. But it is possible to recognise the basic features of organizations, and necessary to do so, and to see also that certain types of organizations (such as profit-making organizations, voluntary organizations, employment organizations) have further general features.

Every real organization is different in some respects from every other, but each, whatever its field and type, has certain basic features which may be recognized and formulated, and which must be taken into account in decisions about organization structure and change. Because each organization is particular and idiosyncratic, so are the solutions to its problems, including its problems of design. There is no set of 'principles of organization' that is generally applicable to give such solutions—such a claim would be refuted by our everyday experience of organizations. But if the general basic features are identified and the proper inferences drawn from them, two virtues follow.

In the first place, the complexity that is a real organization is put into perspective. It *is* complex, but not infinitely so. It is essential not to over-simplify; at the same time, the fact that the complexity is not beyond our grasp can be recognized. Secondly, a way of identifying design problems is given, so that the decisions to be made in a specific set of circumstances can be pinpointed, effective comparisons may be made with other situations, and the effects of the determinants and constraints that follow from the presence of basic features can be allowed for.

It is becoming increasingly obvious that if organizations are to remain effective, they must change, and their changes must be by design as much as possible, and not by default. Three things are needed if this is to be achieved. One is that the basic features of organization and human behaviour must be identified and understood, since these determine what can and what cannot be deliberately designed; they must be taken into account if decisions about organization design are to be competent. It is no use making up new organization designs, or planning re-organization, in the absence of an awareness of what must exist, what factors must be accepted as always present in practice.

In addition, the ability to communicate accurately what the organization design means to the people in it is needed, and this ability must be developed for as yet there is no generally established accurate terminology or language in the subject of organization and management.

Thirdly, there must be an awareness of all the salient factors in the organization and its situation, not just those factors that are explicit or causing trouble. The questions and problems that often are not adequately formulated or recognized (more than vaguely discerned) must be exposed and communicated.

In practice there often seems to be a lack of competence in the design of organizations. It is not so much a lack of competence in certain aspects of design—perhaps a basic structure, a policy, or a technological feature—but a lack of comprehensive competence. Many otherwise well-laid schemes fail in practice because certain perhaps rather hidden but nevertheless vital dimensions of the situation have not been recognized, or, if they have been, have not been dealt with at the same level of competence as the others. Sometimes technically-trained managers for example have learned to consider the economic dimension as well as the purely technical when considering some change or other, but the human social dimension may be ignored or dealt with naïvely and superficially. Sometimes a design for change is an excellent one in terms of the department or circumstances for which it has been devised, but leads to problems of relationship between that department and the rest of the organization. Sometimes the policies and procedures that exist, or the style in which things are done, are not recognized as being as structural in their effects as the more obvious element of structure, and as a result they come into conflict with changes that are made without a consideration of those effects.

I occasionally come across an inhibiting feeling that attention to organization design is somehow 'inhuman'. The idea that people can be 'designed' may be anathema, but once it is recognized that organization is a vehicle for human beings to use, then the design of organizations becomes a matter of concern to us all. Organization is a system for enabling people to reach or attempt to reach certain objectives, and it involves the use of resources to carry out activities towards those objectives. The more effective this system is then the more effective and less wasteful is its use of resources, especially human resources, provided the objectives to which the system is geared are themselves appropriate. If these objectives are appropriate, and for this the development of the proper process for deciding them is important, there is no basic conflict between organizational effectiveness and due regard for human beings, as individuals and in general.

To someone working in an organization, the subject is concrete and real, the everyday and pressing context of his activities and often in fact of a considerable part of his life. There is available a great deal of literature, and exhortation, about management and organization in general, but what the person in the organization wants above all is comment about his specific organization and its particular problems. Only he can make this kind of comment however, but his understanding and his attitude of mind can be assisted and strengthened if he has developed an analytical approach which links together his point of view, his observation, and the information that is available about the subject.

In many organizations today there is a considerable flow of opinion and criticism, often from younger people who are well-educated and equipped with an analytically-trained intellect. If management is to meet this kind of criticism, to turn it into the kind of constructive challenge that enhances the viability and effectiveness of the organization, then they also must be able to develop the same kind of approach.

The need for knowledge about organization design—what can be designed deliberately, what factors must be taken into account, what cannot be designed but can only be responded to—is increasing. Much interest is now developing in the subject in other fields than the industrial. The development of new organizations and the introduction of management techniques is going on very rapidly in the social and medical services, institutions of all kinds, universities, government bodies and so on, and this is widening very rapidly the testing-out of ideas of organization and management, away from the relatively narrow industrial field. The sense of a more general understanding is emerging, together with the recognition that some of the established 'principles' of management are much more specific and limited to the industrial context than perhaps has been realized in the past.

At the same time, the idea that the industrial organization or the hospital, for example, can be considered as a single organizational entity in all respects has been questioned. There is often far more difference between the research department of an industrial firm and the same firm's production department (in terms of kind of structure, style of management, policies and procedures) or between the medical side of a hospital's organization and the administrative side, than there is between the industrial firm as a whole and the hospital as a whole. On the other hand, both of these are examples of employment organizations. They have very different functions, but there is an element of identicality in that both employ people and pay wages and salaries; both are used by people as a means of earning their livings.

Many powerful techniques of organization and management have been developed, but over and over again the introduction of these techniques exposes more fundamental inadequacies in the organization than can be dealt with through the medium of the techniques *per se*. This sometimes (unfairly) brings the technique concerned into disrepute, or, more constructively, leads to a recognition of the need for more fundamental knowledge and less reliance on techniques as 'solutions to problems'.

Another pressure towards better organization design comes from the recognition that the real source of effectiveness, and the real limit to effectiveness, is people, with organization as the vehicle for their efforts. The vehicle may enhance or inhibit their efforts, but it cannot replace them. People are becoming more educated, more demanding and in a sense more powerful, more capable of identifying organizational faults and criticizing them. People expect better organization design; the experience of trying to do work in a responsible way in spite of the inadequacies of the organization is familiar but this kind of situation is increasingly challenged.

A third reason for interest in design is that change is being experienced today in many organizations as the normal and continuous situation, not the occasional or abnormal. This means that organization must be studied as a process, evolving or degenerating in a quasi-biological way in relationship with its environment and in its internal relationships. It means that organizations must be deliberately designed for change, not just to respond to change but to take the initiative in meeting and steering change.

In summary, all these reasons, and others, indicate the need for organization design knowledge, and for the development of an analytical approach to the study of organization design. It is worth emphasizing that the subject is a practical one, in some ways rather like engineering or medicine. Actual organizations exist and evolve or degenerate in many fields, and, like real engineering or medical situations each one is different in some degree from each other. Certain common factors and ubiquitous properties however appear in all organizations, and certain more fundamental subjects underpin the practical phenomena. A knowledge of these factors and properties and their implications is an essential precursor to effective organization design.

PART I
Basic features of organizations

I.1 General considerations

In launching into a description of the basic features of all organizations there is an immediate problem, that of seeing how and where to start. The concept of organization is obviously not a simple one, and there are various different ways in which the subject may be viewed, no one way being fully adequate by itself. But each time I have listened to people from any field of organization discussing the subject deeply, certain generally-agreed points have eventually emerged.

One point is that real organizations are more than just happenings. They have been set up or have developed to do something, to achieve something, to reach some kind of goal; they are *for* something. Sometimes what they were originally for, or should now be for, has been lost sight of; sometimes the people who work in it are not clear about what their organization is for, or are clear but do not fully agree with it. Sometimes the way the organization is structured or managed is no longer as relevant as it should be to what the organization is supposed to be for. Nevertheless, the presence of objective or objectives is a feature of the real organization, whatever the status of that 'objective'.

Another fact is that organizations involve people. We perhaps recognize a special case—the 'one-man band'—but the general view is that of the involvement of people, in the plural, with interaction between them, communication, co-ordination, sometimes interference and conflict, as inevitable features therefore of this aspect of organization.

A further point that always emerges is that organizations do something about their objectives, whether or not what they do is particularly effective. This is then qualified by the observation that it is not actually organizations that do something, but the

B

people in them (though this comment begs the question of the meaning of the term 'organization'). People in organizations carry out activities which should have some connection with what the organization is for—this is the usual final form of the observation.

It is also recognized that organizations exist in environments which are significant to them, with which they interact or with which they must relate in some way or another. This is usually expressed in terms of the objectives of the organization and some of the constraints on them. The organization's objectives involve it in trading with a market, giving services to the public, fighting an enemy, and so on; these are all statements of relationship between the organization and a particular part of its environment. In order to survive, however, the organization must relate with other parts of its environment, with the suppliers of its raw materials, the finance it needs, the people to replace those who retire or are lost in some other way, and also with those features like the law and the general social setting which limit the organization's freedom of action.

These observations give a practical framework to a description of the basic features of any organization. People in the organization carry out activities, or work, in some kind of organized way, towards certain objectives. These several objectives add up eventually to the objectives of the organization as a whole (or they should do) and the objectives of the organization as a whole are concerned with and affected by the relationship between the organization and its environment. This appears to be so, whether the initiative for the determination of the objectives of the organization comes from the environment or from internal considerations.

What we must examine therefore are the basic features of:—

> objectives in the organization;
> work and people in the organization;
> the organization and its environment.

Words and perceptions

Before going any further into the subject, it is worth tackling a general issue in all considerations of organization design, that of words and perceptions. I sometimes feel that many of the people I meet in organizations are capable of talking effectively about everything else but their work and their organization. I also observe often that when people really set out to discuss their work and organizational problems deeply, they discover after a while that they need to go back and clarify the terms they are using, and eventually identify the concepts for which those terms are the 'verbal labels', before they can usefully continue their discussion. Organization is an everyday subject, part of everyone's experience, and not a special science in which a particular technical language has developed. Because this is so, there is nearly always a problem in the choice of words in communicating about organizations and their workings, and we should always keep this in mind if serious misunderstandings and wrong assumptions are to be avoided. This is a vital point when it comes to organization design. Looking back over my own experience, I believe that often the most useful assistance I have given to organizations has been in helping people in them to deal with their semantic problems in order to clarify their concepts of what they were dealing with. They have then been largely capable of thinking out their organization design or the changes they needed to make, for themselves.

This semantic aspect of organization design is not an easy matter. Before any question of organization design or indeed any other kind of design can be dealt with, it is necessary to identify what is basic in the subject under consideration. A knowledge of what must be involved and must not be ignored in design, of the 'givens', is essential for effective design. In other words, the starting point for design is understanding, and to understand anything we must examine it, look at it, analyse it. People often talk about looking at organizations, to examine their various parts and operations in order to understand how they work, what they are, how they change and how to deal with the problems they meet in them. Most of the important aspects of organizations however cannot be seen; we can read about them, listen to what people tell us about them, try to understand what is going on in them by asking questions and listening to the answers we get, but we cannot 'see' them. Thus our ability to examine organizations and to understand them depends very much on our ability to talk about them and to listen accurately to what others say about them. The process of examining an organization is largely verbal rather than visual.

A problem however is that many of the words we need to use in this subject have different meanings for different people, or even when we think they have the same meaning we are often not absolutely confident that this is so. In addition, there is often a multiplicity of terms available for broadly similar features. The essential issue is that concepts must be clarified; once this is done, the choice of the particular term that is to stand for the concept becomes less critical and less emotional. 'Why not use a dictionary?' is sometimes asked. The reason becomes obvious as soon as this is attempted—on the whole, dictionary definitions are descriptions of the usage of terms, not definitions of concepts, and thus they do not deal with the problem we face in this subject.

As to the choice of terms, there are two courses open to us. One is to coin new words, the other to employ existing words in a more limited way than in common usage. The first course produces the problem of jargon, the second sometimes leads to arguments about appropriateness of the term, or its strained use. Nevertheless, the second course is taken here, because in my experience it seems the lesser evil.

Another issue is that of our perceptions—of *how* we see organizations and the various aspects of them. I often hear arguments going on between people in the same organization because they see a common situation or problem in different lights. 'If you were in my job you wouldn't see the problem like that' is a very common assertion. Very often the semantic problem is present at the same time, and a real non-communication then exists between the protagonists. The personal viewpoint of an individual may be highly subjective and biased; it will be affected by his particular job or function and its relationship with the subject under consideration. We therefore should not expect different people to have the same view, and should recognize the need to reconcile different views, not by denying the validity of one or more of them but by understanding why they are different and seeing what is commonly agreed.

In addition, things in organizations are very rarely what they seem to be at first sight. What we read about an organization, in its policies and rules, organization charts and procedures, is one thing. But what the organization is really like may be quite another. People may tell us a great deal about an organization, or about a problem in it, but what they tell us may depend very much on who they are, what their job is in the organization or what their attitude is to the problem. The official statements of the organization structure and its policies and procedures may be a long way from reality.

Because of these factors (not faults—they are the result of normal human behaviour) we should always try to improve our ability to 'see things straight' in an organization before we make decisions about changes we want to achieve, or decide how to deal with a problem. In order to do this we should follow a systematic process of improving our understanding of the situation. We might begin by taking the official statements of what the situation is supposed to be but we should then compare this with personal views of the situation always taking more than one if this is possible, in order to see what agreement there is between them, to cancel out the inevitable personal bias as far as possible.* What we should be aiming at is as clear a view of the situation as we can get; how accurate and confident we can be depends on how much time we have and how open and honest the people who can tell us about what is going on are prepared to be.

* *Exploration in Management* (Brown, Heinemann 1960, Pelican 1968) sets this process out using the terms 'manifest', 'assumed', 'extant' and then 'requisite'.

I.2 Objectives of organizations

Returning now to the things that must be examined, the first consideration is of what the organization is for, what its objectives are.

The presence of the objective or objectives is a general feature of all organization; it is a central issue. Organizations have objectives, however they have been established and whatever they mean to different people in the organization. All work involves objectives, whether this is explicitly recognized or not, and all work in an organization should be linked through its objectives with the objectives of the organization as a whole. Without the concept of objective, the analysis of work or task is inadequate and unsatisfactory, and the organization as a whole is without a focus. The relationship between the organization and its environment is both affected by and provides some of the determinants of the objectives of the organization.

In a sense, 'objectives' should come first, and 'organization' follow as a consequence of these objectives. The answers to the vital questions of what is effective work, how should the organization be structured, what are the proper criteria of performance, all depend on the identification of objectives. Indeed, the basic justification for organization in the first place is that there are desirable objectives which cannot be reached by the efforts of individuals in isolation; they infer organization by their nature, because they need, for their attainment, resources beyond those of strength, skill, judgment, time, material, money and so on possessed by individuals or capable of being used by individuals in isolation.

Organization design begins with the identification of organizational objectives; there is no rational way of devising what the main structure of an organization should be, without an understanding of what the organization is for and what it is trying to achieve. It is essential therefore to be clear, not only about what an organization's objectives are, but about the concept of 'objective'.

The choice of the term objective here is almost an arbitrary one—it is a curious and probably significant thing that in every language of which I have any knowledge there appear to be literally dozens of words or expressions that stand for this concept, or for something like it. Purpose, goal, target, function, reasons, intention, aim, task are some of the English terms. Each one probably has a slightly different shade of meaning from the others, but I do not find much consistent agreement as to what these differences are. This suggests that the concept 'objective' is likely to be a complex one, as well as an important one.

Looking at objectives conceptually then, there appear to be three basic kinds:—

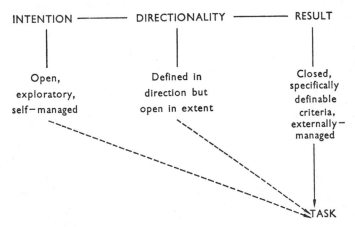

Figure 1—Objectives

One I will describe as 'intention', and examples at the level of the organization as a whole are:—

Our objective is profitability.
Our objective is to do fundamental research.
Our objective is to provide an effective social service.
Our objective is survival.

These may be extremely important statements. They tell us what the organization is for, or what the task is in aid of; people may decide whether or not to join the organization, or to support it, on the basis of such objectives, whether or not to take on the task. But however well this kind of objective is communicated, it does not in itself give a starting point for the allocation of resources, or for planning, or for organization design, or for managing work. This is because what the statement of intention means in terms of action, in terms of tasks, is a matter of conjecture, or arbitrary decision—there is no way in which this arbitrariness can be removed, save by redefining the objective in a different form. There is no rational way in which resources can be allocated, and different people will have different views as to what needs to be done, and what the priorities should be, to meet such objectives. Management in such circumstances can only be by trust (or argument) rather than on a basis of rationality, and there are almost bound to be disagreements about performance between managers and subordinates unless these consequences of objectives defined at the level of 'intention' (however elegant that definition is) are fully understood and accepted.

Of course, activities relating to such objectives can be defined, and resources can be allocated and their use effectively controlled, but the decisions about what these activities should be, about what resources are needed, about delegation, are open to challenge— they cannot be substantiated from the statement of objective; their status does not come from the objective. Because of this, any attempt to manage the situation closely always draws attention to the arbitrariness of such decisions, or to the qualities and values of the person or group making them.

Another kind of objective might be called one of 'directionality'. Examples, at the level of the organization as a whole, are:—

Our objective is to increase profitability.
Our objective is to achieve an increased share of the market.
Our objective is growth.
Our objective is to reduce the number of children in care.
Our objective is to explore this particular sector of technology as far as we can.

This kind of statement is open-ended; it does not indicate how far to go, but it does indicate in which direction action is required. It is a kind of signpost. It allows a rational delineation to be made between what is required to be done and what is not, but it does not indicate how much; the decision will still be an arbitrary one.

The question 'is the organization moving in the required direction?' or 'is the task being progressed?' can be answered, rationally, from the definition of objective, but not the question 'is it moving fast enough?'. The allocation of resources is still largely arbitrary. 'What can be afforded' is likely to be the basis rather than 'what is needed'. Thus performance can properly be assessed only in the light of available resources, and in a situation where those resources have not been allocated as a result of logical inference from desired objective. This is a very familiar situation in many organizations, for many people. Again, there is nothing wrong with it, provided the implications are fully understood and accepted.

The third kind of objective might be called an objective of *result*. This is a statement of what is aimed at, what is to be reached or attempted. It is a closed statement; it indicates the standard of result that is desired. Examples at the level of the organization as a whole might be:—

> Our objective is to achieve a profitability of 16% net return on employed assets this year.
> Our objective is to carry out these research projects by the end of 1973, without exceeding our agreed budget.
> Our objective is to reduce the number of children in care to half its present figure by 1975.

Because this kind of statement is fully closed, a rational determination of what resources are required, what action is needed, what organization structure and what policies must be devised, is possible. The resources necessary if the achievement of the desired result is to be feasible can be identified and the subsequent performance of the person accountable for the results can be assessed on the basis of a comparison between the results actually achieved and those desired, in the light of available resources compared with those identified as necessary.

A major point may now be made—the difference between 'objectives' and 'task objectives'. Task objectives are *always* objectives of the 'result' form, by inference if not by explicit specification. When the basic objective is itself of 'result' form, the problem in defining task objectives is a matter of division of the total into discrete tasks. The bigger problems perhaps occur where the basic objectives are in 'intention' or 'directionality' form, yet must be translated into 'result' form in order that effective action shall be taken about them. The decisions involved cannot be entirely logically based—in brutal terms they are 'arbitrary'. Figure 1 shows the kinds of objective and their implications.

One further point should be made here. As well as the three kinds of objective, whose implications are different and must be understood as such, there is another concept which is often confused with them, leading to inadequate structure and management. This is the concept I will call *determinant*. A determinant, in this context, is something that must be met, must be taken into account, and cannot be ignored. The confusion follows the fact that determinants are sometimes mistaken for 'results to be achieved'. The best way to explain this is by an example. Take the objective (intention) of, say, achieving good relationships between different units in an organization. The statement of objective (of directionality) that could lead to managerial action is 'Improve the relationships'. What this would cost, how long it would take, is a matter of arbitrariness, and commitment to a *result* as a pre-condition obviously is not feasible. A *determinant* of such an objective however would be the development of a number of specific contacts between the units. This is a determinant, for without contacts between the units' people it is obvious that relationships cannot be improved. It is sometimes relatively easy for such determinants to slip into becoming objectives of *result*, and the result is that of trivializing the real objective. In this case, the objective, trivialized, would become that of increasing the number of contacts between the units, missing the real objective of improving the relationships. This degeneration of objectives is a fairly common feature in some organizations, and too often has occurred as the result of applying, without adequate understanding, techniques concerned with the clarification of objectives.

To sum up the vital question of objectives, the issues are as follows:—

There are three linked but different concepts. Their organizational implications are different. At any level, an objective of intention leads to two problems, that of the translation of the objective into appropriate action, and that of the basis of decision as to allocation of resources. Acceptance of the intention, of this kind of objective, is usually readily achieved; the arguments and conflicts are about what tasks should be performed and what resources are needed.

At the other extreme, an objective defined in terms of results leads to a rational identification of the necessary tasks and the resources needed if those tasks are to be feasible. The logic of relationship between resources, tasks and objectives is usually readily recognized; the arguments and conflicts are about the objectives themselves—are these the results we should be aiming at?—and about different views as to adequacy of resources.

In my experience, there is a kind of 'quantum of doubt' or disagreement or conflict in every situation; this quantum can be focused on the objective in the situation, or on the decisions about tasks and resources, or distributed in some way between these factors. What I think matters, for effective organization design, is that this point is recognized and the issues that the doubt and conflict concern are identified, particularly in terms of the responsibilities of the various individuals involved in the situation.

1.3 People and work

The next feature to examine is that of people and their activities, their work—and I am using the term 'work' in a general sense. Whatever an organization is for, it involves people doing something —call it, in general, working. It is worth picking up immediately a design implication from this elementary point. If there is more than one person around in any kind of circumstances, then the freedom of action of the individual is not absolute, but limited by the presence and activities of the other individuals there. This is so whether the other individuals are limiting the freedom of the one by deliberate action or just by their presence. In an organization therefore, whether its structure is formalized or not, and whether or not things are done in a humane and reasonable way, the individual's freedom of action, his autonomy, will always be bounded; it will never be absolute.

In addition, limits or constraints on the activities of the individual come from the individual himself, in terms of his capabilities and also his willingness to act.

Thus there are two sources of limits of freedom:—

those to do with the individual;
those external to the individual.

Nobody can do anything that is beyond their capabilities, physical or mental. There are limits beyond which, whatever incentives or penalties are offered, threatened or applied, the individual cannot or will not go. The individual however exists in a physical and social context which sets external limits to his freedom of action. The physical context which allows human survival and mobility has limits of temperature, pressure, availability of oxygen, noise and so on; the social context involves social limits *per se* (due to the presence and actions of other people) and the economic and organizational limits that are a consequence. The organizational limits come from the kind of work involved (it is never 'any old work', it always has some specific properties and limits) and from the organization structure, policies and procedures that apply in the situation. These two sets of limits or delineation of freedom of action, coming from the work itself and from the organization structure, are not necessarily complementary; they should be, in an ideal organization, but in practice there are always differences. The aim in effective design in this sense is to minimize these differences as far as possible.

The reason why there are differences in practice is that there are other determinants of organization structure than the properties of the work that the organization is set up to do. The personalities involved, the organization's past, the presence of other objectives than those to do with the organization's work or on which the organization's work is based, are examples of these other determinants.

The situational view of work

The concept of work in situational terms obviously contains the sense of desired or required *activity*. But there is a qualification to be made, that perhaps is illuminated by an experience I had years ago when working as a research engineer. I was visited by my research director, who seemed to be in somewhat of a hurry, and told to 'get on with some work'. When I replied that I was in fact working, as I was thinking about a problem in the project with which I was concerned, he replied, 'Well, look as if you're working. I'm bringing a potential customer round in a few minutes and we want to give him a good impression.'

This underlines one basic misconception about work, a misconception that still occurs too often in practice; this is that work is necessarily a visible activity, something that can be seen being done. A moment's thought indicates however that another kind of activity is also possible and likely, one that cannot be observed directly visually—a mental activity. The qualification therefore is that the concept of activity involves more than physical or observable activity; it includes mental activity, thinking, decision-making, use of judgment or discretion.

The requirement of mental and/or physical activity does not fully describe work however. The question 'what is the activity for?' is as valid and essential as the question 'what is the activity?', and it identifies an aspect of work other than that of activity. This is the aspect of *objective*. Work involves activity or activities that are to some purpose, towards some goal, and this is so even in the extreme case where the purpose is to 'be active', with no other objective; the concepts of activity and objective still stand.

This recognition leads to the observation of another misconception, that work can be rated or valued in terms of the extent or difficulty, value or sense of responsibility in the activities involved. This is not so; the proper criterion of activity is *relevance to objective*; no other criterion is valid. Yet there are still examples of work evaluation techniques in use which are based only on the properties of the activities in the work situation and not with the relationship between the activities and their objective. The basic value of an activity is in its relevance to its objective, not in its intrinsic properties of difficulty, quantity, responsibility.

The activities that should be planned, designed, are therefore those that are relevant to objectives. The activities that can be carried out however are those allowed by the available *resources*. Resources determine what is feasible. These three linked features—objectives, activities, resources—give the basic concept of work, in situational terms, and by recognizing them we are given a fundamental way of identifying a work situation, or role, or a task. The task of the organization as a whole can be described in terms of the use of resources to carry out activities towards certain objectives, and in the same way the work situation of an individual may be identified. In setting up a work role, in delegating work, in any communication about work, these three basic items must be involved and their interaction understood. In terms of organization design, these are the three basic features in every work situation, at any level, which must be identified and dealt with in some way. Figure 2 shows them and their interaction.

Organizations are set up or evolve because there are certain objectives that cannot be met by the activities of individuals in isolation. This is because in order to reach them, activities need to be carried out that are beyond the resources of strength, skill, judgment, money, materials, time and so on that the individual possesses or could use by himself. Organization's objectives require activities to be carried out that are beyond one person's efforts. Thus in an organization, there is or should be a relationship between the activities of every person in it and those of every other person;

whatever the form or way of working in the organization each person should be carrying out activities leading towards objectives that are related to the organization's objectives, and in order to do this each person should have available to him the access to the resources that make those activities feasible. A serious problem in some organizations is that the resources available in the organization as a whole are not effectively allocated into the areas of work where they are needed. This has just as bad an effect as a basic lack of resources. Sometimes this situation is compounded by lack of information about what resources are available, and it is tragic to

OBJECTIVE

Relevance

ACTIVITIES

Feasibility

RESOURCES

Figure 2—Work analysis

see, occasionally, important work inhibited by lack of resources, when the organization possesses the necessary resources somewhere but has neither the information nor the ability to make them available at the work point.

These features of a work situation—objectives, activities, resources—may be defined and communicated, in the form of task-definitions, or comprehensively as role-definitions. In real situations however we are concerned with more than the definition of work, or the design of roles. The prime concern is in getting work done, and work is actually done by people. The relationship between the person and the features of the work situation is therefore of major interest. This relationship is not a simple one. In the first place, as already indicated, work is not a single factor issue. I find that it is often a dangerous over-simplification to regard people as relating with work, or motivated in work, or responsible for work—what is more accurate is the recognition that people are likely to have a differential relationship with work, depending on which of the factors is being considered. The person carrying out a task may be very happy indeed about the objective in the situation, but not so sanguine about the resources that are available. He may approve of the activities that are required, but disagree with their objective.

Furthermore, the person who is carrying out the work may be clear about the objective in that work, about the available resources and about the appropriate activities, *from the work point of view*, but may have other objectives—personal ones—that interact or perhaps even interfere with the work objectives. He may have his own way of acting, which tends to modify the activities initially defined, and his ability to use the resources available to him in the work situation is not necessarily identical with the implications of the presence of those resources.

These features can be seen easily in the situation where a different person takes over a piece of work previously carried out by someone else. The requirement in the work situation, in terms of objectives, activities and resource availability does not change at any rate to begin with, but the actual way in which the new person relates with these requirements will be different, to some extent. The same resources will be used differently. The same required activities will be carried out in a different personal way, and although the work objective has not changed, the personal objectives are different to some extent, inevitably, so that the interaction between work-objectives and personal objectives is different. The thing that really matters is not that the new person is relating with the work in a different way, but whether the way he is relating with the work requirements reinforces them or is in conflict with them.

The set of relationships between the person and the features of the work situation is thus one of duality. On the one hand there is the set of relationships with the organizationally-required features, relationships which should be ones of knowledge as to what those features are, based on their adequate definition and communication to the person. On the other hand there is the purely personal set of relationships, determined by who the particular person is, affected by all the other factors in that person's state, factors other than those to do with the work itself. The personality, the skills, intelligence, attitude of mind, and the cultural pressures and pressures resulting from membership of other organizations than the one of which the work being considered is a part, are all factors affecting this other set of relationships.

An understanding of this duality leads to the recognition of how to communicate effectively about task or role. In some way or another, each of the three basic features of work must be communicated or be capable of being inferred. The objective is one of these features, the access to resources that is allowed is another, and the activities required is the third. This is not all however. The communications must be such as to leave room for the particular person who is to do the work to relate with those features. This means that the communications must indicate the work objective but not deny personal objectives, to define activities required

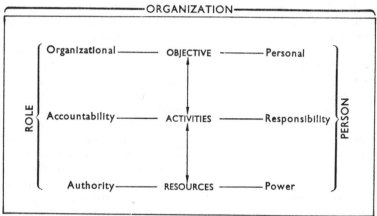

Figure 3—Organization-relationships between people and work

but not so sharply if possible that no room is left for the person to carry out the required activities to some extent in their own way, and to indicate the access to resources that is authorized, without denying that people relate with their resources to some extent in a personal way. These requirements mean basically that it is the boundaries that must be communicated, within which the person who will do the work will decide for himself how to do it, will use his own judgment, his own discretion, and which at the same time protect the organization from excessive idiosyncrasy in that person.

In order to describe these various relationships, some organizationally determined or agreed, and others purely personally determined, it is helpful to use different terms for each of them, as I have done in Figure 3. Their interaction is so important in practice, and it is necessary to be able to refer to them without going into full

C

description every time. The problem of words, mentioned earlier, hits hard here because some people have very strong feelings about the proper meaning of terms such as 'authority' and 'responsibility'. Once again however, since it is concepts that are the analytical tools we need, not words, and these concepts are the relationships that have been identified, the choice of words is not so important as long as we are consistent in their use. There just is not a generally agreed set of specific terms or expressions for these vital relationships, and so I have elected to use terms in a way that is as near to their general usage as possible.

The term 'authority' stands for the access to resources permitted by the organization, and 'power' for the personal link with those resources—the ability and willingness to use them. This use of the term 'authority' is in line with practice—if authority is not 'access to resources' then it is not meaningful—and links with the sociological concept of 'legitimacy'. The use of the term 'power' is consistent with the more general case of the combined power of subordinates to limit the effective use of authority by managers.

'Accountability' is the organizational requirement for activities to be carried out, and 'responsibility' is the term for the personal way of carrying them out. 'Organizational objective' and 'personal objective' are the third pair. Using these terms, the proper situation of the person in a role can be described as one in which the work objectives are clear and at least not in conflict with the personal objectives, where the limits of accountability are understood and responsibility is present within them, and the person has the power to use the resources to which the authority in his role gives him access.

The process view of work

Work as a process may be described in various ways. There are technological processes, control processes, managerial processes, communication processes for example, and many others. All these processes have structural implications and they all have interaction with the situational structure of the organization. A general way of describing work in process terms that is very helpful in allowing the link with the situational structure to be explored is to recognize it in general as a decision process. The action of work has to be carried out, but what that action has to be must be determined in some way or another. The carrying out might be described as the *implementation* stage of the whole process, the determination stage being called *decision-making*. Whatever the subject, every decision process contains these stages of decision-making and implementation. (I suspect however that occasionally the natural order is reversed, and decisions are 'made', or rationalised, after implementation.)

Decision-making is not a simple stage. One element is *analysis*, the recognition of the circumstances, the factors, the data, to be taken into account. Sometimes decisions appear to be made on the basis of individual intuition, or even randomly, in the absence of recognition of what data and knowledge are available. Sometimes indeed decisions appear to be made almost instantaneously—'snap decisions'—but in fact, however minimal, inadequate or unrecognized it is, analysis of some kind is always an element of the whole process.

The second element is the development and taking of the decision. (This is often described as decision-making, and sometimes misconceived as the whole process.) If all the necessary information were available in an appropriate form, there would be no need for a decision but only for the application of logic or mathematics. Decisions are needed when there is inadequacy of data, and thus decisions always involve assessment, judgment, uncertainty and risk. A decision cannot be right or wrong, but only more or less appropriate and effective in the circumstances.

This element of the whole process is often a complex one. In most cases it is a kind of 'shaping' process. A decision is proposed, thought about, commented on, modified, argued out—shaped— and eventually crystallized and formulated. This is so whether the process goes on entirely in the mind of an individual or involves interaction with other people.

Implementation, the other stage of the whole process, always involves the commitment and use of resources. The process as a whole is only as effective as its implementation stage. The implementation stage itself then involves a whole set of consequential decision processes—analysis, decision-making and implementation —and so on until the final results are achieved, the whole extended process ended.

As well as these hierarchical consequential decision processes in the implication stage, each decision process as a whole is likely to be iterative. Feedback from implementation or part-implementation forms part of the data whose analysis may lead to a modification of the decision itself. In the decision-making part of the whole process, the exploring of options may affect the view of the data. In fact, the whole process is one of considerable complexity, and has been comprehensively studied.* What I am concerned with here are the basic organizational features of the process, since as well as implications for managerial style, leadership and participation, which will be discussed later, there are vital structural implications to be observed also. People who make certain decisions are not necessarily those who will implement them. The contribution of people with valuable information in the analytical stage needs to be arranged, structured, if it is to be achieved. Authority to implement may not be the same as authority to investigate or analyse, or authority to make the decisions which will subsequently be implemented, and any distinctions of this sort need to be clarified and communicated adequately—these are structural comments.

In very basic terms indeed, the various stages of the whole process offer very different possibilities or options for structure and design. There is a whole range of ways in which decisions may be made, from the autocratic, dictatorial, unilateral way (which may be extremely effective in appropriate circumstances, and completely disastrous in others) to the democratic, egalitarian, multilateral (which may be essential if co-operation is to be achieved in some circumstances, yet may be unreasonably slow, effective or not effective, depending on the situation) at the other extreme.

Compared with this range of possibilities for decision-making, and their advantages and disadvantages, there is only one basic way to implement decisions. If more than one person is involved, implementation requires differentiation of activity, of task, of role, and therefore of authority and accountability; it involves therefore a hierarchical structure. If only one person is involved, it nevertheless requires activities to be carried out in a certain order, and in this sense it is still hierarchical. The reason for this is obvious, once the existence of more than one stage in the total process is recognized; it is that the doing of work, at any level, requires a certain ordering of activities and of availability and use of resources. Tasks are formed of sub-tasks, objectives lead to sub-objectives, the doing of work is a hierarchical process. Figure 4 sets these features out in a diagram.

Perhaps we should look at the term 'hierarchical' for a moment, because it seems to cause a lot of difficulty and misunderstanding.

---

* For example, *Decision Making: Selected Readings* (Edwards and Tversky, Penguin 1967).

Much time is wasted in debating whether organizations can be non-hierarchical, whether bureaucracies are inevitably hierarchical, whether hierarchical relationships are the antithesis of democratic ones. None of these questions is meaningful unless the process of work is properly understood and until the term 'hierarchical' is defined and separated from the unfortunate connotations that often go along with it.

The concept is that of a set or system of persons or things ranked in some kind of order, and it is the ranking feature that distinguishes a hierarchy from other kinds of sets.

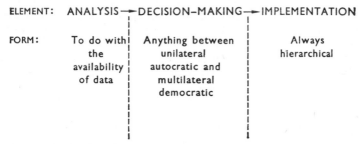

Figure 4—The decision process

Random vehicles on a road are not a hierarchy. If however the particular vehicles are obliged to pass a given point in a certain order of precedence, then this set of vehicles becomes a hierarchy. If the vehicles are coupled together, there is then a hierarchy. Random general managers, unit managers and section managers do not form a hierarchy (though the concepts do). If however a particular general manager A has a subordinate unit manager B who in turn manages a subordinate C, then the A-B-C set is a hierarchy, in this case one of authority and accountability, and corresponding hierarchies of objectives, tasks, level of work and so on should be discernible.

If an organization in which work is done, whatever its form, is examined, the existence of a number of hierarchies may be recognized. The hierarchies may be to do with the work itself (with the planning of the work, the control, the review of the work, the accounting for the work and for the use of resources) or with the organization itself (the managerial hierarchy, the hierarchy of special knowledge, the leadership hierarchy).

The identification of hierarchies in organizations and how they relate together or interact is essential; there is a detrimental effect when different hierarchies (or their implications) in the same organization are out of step or out of phase one with another.

The whole process then involves two main forms, for decision-making and implementation, and therefore two main sets of behaviour. If more than one person is involved, two main relationships will need to develop. One sharply visible example of this duality of relationship amongst the same people is seen in American football, at any rate as observed through European eyes. At various points in the game, the action stops and the players of one team huddle together, discussing tactics and then deciding the next stage of the play. The huddle is manifestly a physical one, but the relationships are participative; they are quite different from those when play is resumed. Now the group breaks into action, and the individual players take up their distinctive positions, their individual action roles. There is no real conflict between a democratic way of making decisions and the hierarchical nature of their implementation; the difficulty may be in the shift of style that is needed from one stage of the total process to the other. It may be easier to accept the need for clear hierarchical structure of implementation when decision-making itself is unilateral and non-democratic, but to the extent that unilateral exercise of authority and non-participatory decision-making is not acceptable in an organization the difficulty must be understood and overcome if that organization is to be effective.

These two sets of elements of work—the situational set of objectives, activities and resources, and the process set of analysis, decision-making and implementation—make up the content of *role*. Whether a role is established in a general way, or as a set of discrete tasks, or whether it has 'just developed', it can be described in terms of the objectives in it, the activities involved and the resources available. The action in the role can also be described in terms of analysis, decision-making and implementation, this process being concerned with using resources to carry out activities towards certain objectives.

Objectives have been discussed in some detail; let us also look in a little more depth at resources and activities.

Resources

The allocation of resources in such a way that work is enabled to be done effectively is a key feature of organization design. It is helpful to examine this in more detail. The connection between resources and authority has already been made, and in any question of organization design therefore it is worth recognizing the meaning of resources and the implications of their allocation. It is also necessary to recognize that the nominal allocation of resources, or establishment of authority, may be modified by limitations on their use, often in the form of policies, procedures, or informal constraints, some of which may be hidden. The effective method of allocating resources is to indicate the boundaries of availability; this delineates the range of authority of access to resources available to the person accountable for the work. If there are further limitations on the use of resources, then these should also be communicated as boundaries.

A resource is relative to the circumstances in which it is used or available to be used. A resource that is valuable and effective in one set of circumstances may be useless or even an encumbrance or embarrassment in a different set. For example, money is a valuable resource where it can be used to buy or hire things that are needed, but there are many things that money cannot buy or hire. A particular kind of machinery, or a particular professional skill, may be a vital resource until the product changes, or the clients' needs change; the machinery or skill may then become redundant. The concept 'resource' is not the simple one suggested by the word, but one of relationship between whatever is loosely thought of as 'resource' and the circumstances wherein it is to be used.

This simple point has an immediate implication for organization design. In an effective organization, as work requirements in a role change, the allocation of resources to that role will also be changed; a change of accountability warrants a change of authority. This obvious point is sometimes not acted on however, because there is present a feeling, however irrational, that the status of a person in a role is determined by the quantity of resources available. Thus an increase of available resources is acceptable; a decrease, which may be equally valid, is not. This problem may be exacerbated if evaluation methods or payment policies are used which are also based on the extent or value of resources controlled by the individual, rather than on the quality of the individual's use of those resources. What is needed here is a better understanding of the relationship between the individual and his work, so that effectiveness in work becomes the criterion of performance, or status, or pay, rather than the apparent 'size' of the role as indicated by the quantity of resources available in it.

The next point about resources is that there is a difference between resources which are used directly, in doing work, and resources which are used to obtain other resources. If we called the first kind *working resources*, then it may be observed that all work, at any level, and of any kind, inevitably involves three broad elements of resource—time, and the physical and human elements. These three, in some kind of combination, make up the working resource which is needed, or available, for the particular piece of work or task concerned. The human element for example, without time, is as meaningless as the physical element without a human being to relate with it. It is essential therefore if work is to be done that all the elements of working resource are allocated; any deficiency in one element will prejudice the whole.

I have not yet mentioned an obvious resource—money. But money is not a working resource. As a resource it enables us to obtain the working resources we need, or can afford, in order to make our work feasible. Some of our working resources cannot be obtained through the medium of money, and others we may lay hands on by other methods than purchase or hire. Money is an *enabling resource*. As a design feature, the allocation of financial authority—authority to use the enabling resource of money—is obviously significant. What is often not so obvious is that the delegation of financial authority is not really as important as it is felt to be in some organizations. The basic delegation of authority must be in terms of access to working resources; financial authority in a role is only fundamentally required if it is used as the indirect method of gaining access to the necessary working resources, or if the working resources which have been allocated directly are allowed to be changed directly by the occupant of the role.

Another enabling resource is information. There is a problem of terminology here, because a great deal of information in organizations may not be a resource at all, or only a resource when fed into certain roles. It is necessary to distinguish between information that is needed if certain work is to be done (resource) and information that is interesting, fills in the background, and so on. Access to the former is a necessary element in the role; access to the latter may be useful, be valued, enhance the status of the recipient, but is not a necessary enabling resource. Sometimes the latter floods out the former—there is so much information around that the vital information that is a necessary resource cannot get through, or is not noticed.

The enabling resources must be more than present, or available; they must be used, or spent, or translated into working resources or into implications for the use of working resources, if they are to be effective in practice. Access to financial resource without the authority to spend it is meaningless. Access to information, without the ability or training to use it is not of any consequence. I sometimes meet situations however where access to working resources and access to enabling resources are delegated but there is insufficient recognition that there must be some freedom of use of the enabling resources if the authority of access to them is to be effective. If there is hidden constraint on the extent of this freedom, or confusion exists as to how far it extends, then the situation will not be one of good design.

Figure 5 shows the relationship between resources.

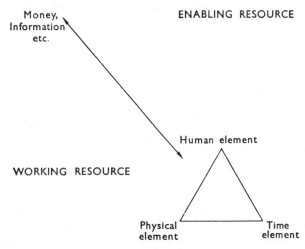

Figure 5—The relationship between resources

Authority and power

Now let us look further at the interaction between authority—the access to resources established in a role, or for a given task, and power—the capacity of the person involved, in terms of ability and willingness to use those resources.

One of the terms—authority—is concerned with something that can be designed, the access to resources that is allowed or established. The other—power—concerns something that cannot be designed, though it can be influenced, but in organization design room must be left for it. In other words, roles must be designed in terms of authority not only commensurate with the work content in the role but in the light of the power to use that authority possessed by the person occupying the role. It is no use allocating authority to someone who lacks the competence or willingness to use it. Nor is it effective or appropriate to allocate authority of access to resources to someone who does not need to use those resources in their work, even though they would be competent to do so.

The design implications then are clear; what causes confusion in practice is confusion in terminology. I am using the two terms as verbal labels for different concepts whose interaction is an important feature in organizations, but there are other terms and expressions used which do not differentiate sufficiently between these two concepts. Whatever terms are used, clarity of the two concepts is essential, and this should be used as a test of the terms that are employed.

In general usage, the terms power, authority, right, influence, perhaps leadership, and others like them apply to people or groups or their roles, and enable them to cause things to be done or prevent things being done, to influence events or to inhibit them. They are to do with achieving action or with preventing action, and must basically therefore be connected with resources, since resources are the determinants of action. Unless the resources needed are to hand, a task cannot be accomplished by the most powerful of men. On the other hand, possession of resources or access to resources is one thing, but the ability to use them is obviously another. If the necessary resources are not available, by possession or by access, then this prevents the task being carried out. But even if they are available, unless the person trying to use them has the ability and willingness to do so, then again the task will not be carried out effectively. Another way of putting this is that the ability and willingness of the person to use resources effectively is one of the necessary resources.

As discussed earlier however, a resource is effective only in relationship to the circumstances in which it is used. If action is to be achieved, or prevented, if tasks are to be carried out, then the resources that are needed *in that situation* must be available, by possession or by access, and the person concerned with the action or accountable for the task must have the ability and willingness to use them in that situation.

In an organization, certain resources are possessed by people themselves, as individuals—their capacity, strength, abilities, talents, sense of responsibility, willingness and motivation are examples. These individual possessions may be augmented or modified when people are in groups—groups possess resources, which may be different from the mere summation of the individuals' resources. Other resources however are made available to people or groups by the organization—deployed into their roles. For example, access to the organization's money, to services, to information and advice possessed by others, to the efforts of other people, to materials and plant, and so on may be arranged. This kind of access to resources which are not one's own possessions but are necessary attributes of one's role—authority—needs to be distinguished from the other kind, the possession of people as individuals or in groups—power. The presence of authority means that an organization has identified in the role of a person or group the access to resources that is needed if they are to carry out their tasks, or indeed get anything done. If authority is to be effective, however, the access to resources which it represents must be effective in the situation for which it is intended, and the person occupying the role, authorized to use the resources available in that role, must have the ability and willingness to do so—the power to do so. For effectiveness, therefore, access to the relevant resources must be provided and there must be personal capacity to use those resources. Appropriate authority must be deployed into roles which must be occupied by people of sufficient power. In order to control resources, the individual must either own them or have access to them in his or her role, and possess the personal attributes that allow him or her to use those resources.

People may increase (or indeed in some instances decrease) their power by association with other people, in groups. Interaction takes place between power and authority not only in the situation of 'individual in role' but also between groups, and this interaction may be one of conflict or co-operation. Co-operation may be dependent on bargaining or negotiation (for which 'consultation' may usefully prepare the way, but is no substitute) and the system of negotiation may be formalized.

A major area of interaction is that between the authority in an organization and the power of individuals and groups occupying roles in it. Unless their power sanctions authority, then authority cannot be effective. The association of employees to forward their personal or group interests gives rise to a separate social system in an organization, with its own structure of roles and relationships, which may be called the 'sanctioning system'.* This may be implicit or explicit, and it runs in parallel with the work organization; an employee may find himself acting in either system at different times.

If a sanctioning system is recognized explicitly, formal mechanisms may be set up, to negotiate or 'legislate' the specific limits of authority in the organization or in groups of organizations, and this should be the basis of works councils and other employee/employer negotiating bodies if they are to be effective. The whole question of interaction between a work organization and the sanctioning system within it, or between an employer and a Trade Union, is a major one, and is not within the scope of this book. The power-authority analysis however can lead to a deeper understanding of such interactions.

Activities

Paradoxically, perhaps, activities seem to be the least important element of work, from the design point of view. Given clarity of objectives and definition of what resources are available, the actual activities can often be left to the individual worker, with boundaries specified organizationally and by training. What must be exposed are any constraints on activities, and sometimes serious problems and conflicts arise in practice because all the constraints or boundaries are not identified; there are some that remain hidden until they are exceeded or ignored, and then the conflicts arise. I frequently meet situations in which people think they have freedom of action, and only discover that this is not so when they have crossed some hidden line; by then however the damage is done, and recriminations follow. Some of the experiments in industrial firms to set up 'profit centres'—roles whose occupants are accountable for the profitability of what they manage and have apparent freedom of action as to how they achieve that profitability, within broad organizational terms of reference—have failed because actions within the profit centre have cut across other accountabilities, other policies and procedures in the larger organization, with the

---

* Others have called it the 'representative system', but this expression can cause confusion because the term representative has another meaning, and the system does not necessarily involve representatives; it is a sanctioning system, whether or not the sanctioning is communicated through representatives. See *Exploration in Management* (Brown, Heinemann 1960, Pelican 1968).

result that the profit centre manager has become frustrated or cynical about the approach, an opposite result from the enhanced motivation that the approach is supposed to achieve.

The real problem of activities is not a design problem, but a problem for the person or group involved in the activities. It is the problem of deciding what to do and how to do it, to use resources in the best way in order to achieve the desired results—it is really the problem of feasibility and relevance. Dealing with this problem is the fundamental requirement placed on the individual or group by the work, the tasks for which they are accountable. In any kind of organization, this is where people show the real value of their contribution; in an employment organization, this is basically what people should be paid for. It is the real human demand in work. Organization design, role definition, task delineation can only identify its boundaries.

I.4 Roles in an organization

General considerations

People do work in an organization because they accept and occupy roles in the organization; they are appointed to positions, take on jobs. Thus the form and description of roles is a major element of organization design. The concept of role has already been touched upon; the work required of the individual, the tasks he is expected to perform, the situation and process he is expected to deal with, with the implications of position, status, relationships, form the content of his role.

In practice, misunderstandings and misconceptions about roles are a common source of difficulty and inadequacy in organizations and in relationships, and so a proper identification of role is very important in organization design.

One feature of a role that needs to be clear is its description. A role must be described appropriately, because it always means more than a statement of position. A role is a set of expectations, placed by the organization (often personified in this context by the manager) on the person in the role. This is so even if the role itself has been created by the person in it; if it is a role in an organization then the organization has recognized it, explicitly or implicitly accepted it, and this recognition implies expectations. These expectations must be communicated to the person in the role. This means that the general statement of role must indicate what the role is for, what its occupant is expected to achieve, what objectives are involved, as well as what activities are required or permitted. The statement must also indicate what access to resources is authorized in the role, and any limits on the way those resources are used. Without such a statement about resources, the definition of role is incomplete, for activities cannot be carried out unless there is access to the resources that make them feasible.

Since a role is related not only to the needs and expectations of the organization but to the properties of its human occupant, these properties must be taken into account if the statement or definition of role is to be effective. The main property of the human being in this context is that of freedom, the ability to use discretion, to make decisions, in fact the inability not to use discretion, whether wisely or unwisely. The form of statement of role must therefore allow the delineation of autonomy, of discretion, to be ascertained; it must be a statement of the boundaries within which the person in the role is free to act, to make decisions which commit resources to use.

The work content of a role is in the form of tasks, allocated into the role from external sources (often the manager) or self-induced by the person in the role. Self-induced tasks are organizationally valid if they come within the limits of the general accountability of the role, set by the organization. Otherwise, appropriately they should be agreed by the manager. Tasks allocated externally come either from or through the manager, or directly, and again, in the latter instance, they should fall within the general accountability of the role if they are to be organizationally appropriate. In each case, therefore, the basic features of tasks should be a matter between the role-occupant and the manager. This point becomes very significant sometimes when there is a multiplicity of tasks in the role, coming from more than one source, and the question of priorities arises. It is essential that difficulties are resolved (or disagreed) between manager and subordinate, rather than just left. If left, they fester, and recriminations are inevitable. If recognized, action one way or the other can be achieved.

The reason why the work content of roles should be in the form of tasks is that for objectives to be acted on, they must be defined as task objectives. If resources are to be used effectively, the tasks involved must be delineated. A meaningful statement of task is always one of closed form, though this is not always explicitly recognized. The task objective, the limits of time, expenditure and use of other resources, the standards of performance in the task, must all be identified in the statement of the task, or discoverable in some way by the person carrying out the task.

One issue that can cause trouble is that of misconception about when a task is completed. The obvious answer is 'when it is finished', but there is more to it than that if the task has been carried out in an organizational context. The task will have been part of a role, and there has been a person involved, occupying the role and with organizational accountability for the task, and a sense of personal responsibility for it also. Resources will have been used in order to carry out the task. The task may therefore have been physically completed, but the accountability remains until the organization (usually through the manager) has responded to that task. The response may be called the task review, and it should include an awareness of the way in which resources have been used as well as of the completion of the task. Review of course may take place simultaneously with completion of the task, but often it does not, and it is essential to be aware that the task—in the sense of account-ability—is not 'completed' until it has been reviewed.

There are often reasons, technical or organizational, why review does not occur as soon as the direct activities involved in carrying out the task cease, and organization design must take these into consideration.

The link with delegation might be touched upon here. Delegation must be of tasks, otherwise it is not effective; it must indicate what is to be achieved or attempted and what resources are allocated to it. Another feature of effective delegation however is that it is consistent, consistent in the sense of the level of the tasks delegated and consis-tent also in the sense of allocation of task itself. Delegation is incon-sistent if widely differing tasks in terms of level are delegated to the same person. It is also inconsistent if the same task is delegated to different people, arbitrarily. The latter amounts to 'divide and rule', and while it may appear to enhance the apparent power of the person delegating, it defeats its objective of getting effective work done through others.

One distinction that must be made in practice (and often is not) is that between a role which involves a multiplicity of tasks and the situation where the individual occupies more than one role. This is important because a great part of the question of behaviour, accountability and authority hangs on it. In the situation of a role involving a multiplicity of tasks, the problems are those of relative priorities between the tasks, distribution of effort, resources, between the tasks. If the person in the role cannot resolve these problems, then the manager related with that role should do so, however complicated the problems are.

When, however, more than one role is involved (as, for example, when a senior manager in an industrial firm is also a member of the Board of Directors, or when in an organization for professional work a manager is also a professional adviser) the problems are not only those within the roles themselves, but between the roles. Which role takes precedence? Which role invests the occupant with what authority, and how can confusion in the minds of other people be avoided? In this situation, these questions can only be dealt with appropriately by someone whose own role is linked, with authority, with the roles whose interaction is causing the problem. This higher-level role is the 'cross-over' role*; it is in the position of being able to relate with the area of difficulty in an effective way, and it is not always the role of immediate manager, but sometimes far removed from the level of the problem. It is a feature of good design that the cross-over point be identifiable and as near to the problem as possible.

A different problem exists when the roles are in different organizations; no cross-over role is possible of course in these circumstances (unless the different organizations are subsidiaries of a larger entity). The relationship between the roles in this case is determined and regulated by the relationship between the organizations, and this may be one in the wider realms of politics, economics and so on. An example is where a person who occupies a role in an employment organization is also a member of a Trade Union, or a professional institution. The questions of priority between these roles, of loyalties and responsibilities in a situation of conflicting interests between the roles, can only be resolved either by personal or by inter-organizational means.

The general question of whether a person can satisfactorily occupy more than one role seems to be coming up more frequently as time goes on. For example, can a person with special knowledge, whose main job is to carry out tasks in his own particular unit, also act as a consultant to other units in an organization? Can a manager carry other kinds of responsibility than the managerial? Can a senior manager also act as a member of a Board of Directors?

The answer to questions of this nature is in the affirmative, provided that there is clarity about what the different roles are; particularly in terms of authority and accountability. This means that the various roles cannot be occupied simultaneously by the one person—it is essential to be able to identify the role being occupied at the time, and to differentiate from it the other role or roles which the person might occupy at other times or in other circumstances. The behaviour of the person involved must be related to the role occupied at the time, and the clarity and differentiation of role

* This expression was first used in the Glacier Project research.

D

must be apparent to those affected by the roles as well as to the person occupying the roles.

Of course, the best way to achieve differentiation of role is for individual people to be associated with single roles, but however theoretically desirable this is, it seems to me to be quite unrealistic in many situations to limit people and roles in this way. The human resource that is the person in the one role may be of great value in other roles, and the organization may not be able to afford recognizing this and acting on it.

What matters is role clarity, for without this serious confusion and difficulty will arise, with conflicts about authority and accountability then becoming almost inevitable. The basic understanding required is that multiplicity of tasks does not of itself indicate more than one role; the sources of tasks must be identified to establish this. The distinction is very important when the question of the authority or autonomy of the person involved is considered; authority to decide what effort to put into tasks that are competing with each other for attention is one thing, to mediate between competing roles is quite another.

Behind all this understanding, which helps to differentiate behaviour between roles if they require it, is the fact that nevertheless the same person is involved. Particularly if the person has a strong personality and relatively set behaviour pattern, it must be recognized that this will go against the differentiation that may be required. The whole situation therefore can be understood only in terms of the different roles and their implications for behaviour, in relationship with the one person and his inherent pattern of behaviour.

An important point to be considered in the design of a role is the distinction between pressure of work and level of work.

What causes pressure of work on the occupant of a role is the presence of tasks in that role. The presence of tasks may affect the role-occupant in various ways—a single task may involve a quantity of work such that the role-occupant feels under pressure, or the pressure may come from the fact that the role contains a multiplicity of tasks and the pressure may be due less to the task that is being carried out than to the presence of tasks that are not being worked on at a given point in time (because activity of the role-occupant can only be on one task at a time, however intermittent).

Whether a certain pressure of work is tolerable to the role-occupant appears to be a function not only of the pressure itself but of how it is established. For instance, in general a person will tolerate a higher level of pressure if it is self-induced than if it is totally determined from above. A person at a high pressure of work may be broken by an extra task imposed externally, long before the effect would occur if the extra task were taken on as a result of his own decision. Delegated discretion as to the programming or priorities of tasks within a role appears therefore to be a factor affecting tolerable pressure of work.

Level of work is to do with the responsibility in the work, and it causes pressure of a different kind on the occupant of the role. If the level of work is higher than the capacity of the person to do it, then anxiety and eventually perhaps paralysis or abdication will occur; if it is lower, boredom and frustration are the likely results.

Thus both pressure of work and level of work produce stress in the role-occupant if there is significant mismatch between them and the capacity of the person in the role, but the kinds of stress are different. I occasionally meet situations of low pressure of work in association with high level of work, or high pressure of work at too low a level, with very serious effects on the person concerned, and such combinations should be avoided by good design.

In some roles, the work content is inherently difficult; this may be the case for example when the work is of a high level scientific or professional nature, stretching to the utmost the capacity of knowledge and skill of the person in the role. In other roles, however, the work itself may not be of particular difficulty for the person concerned, but the organizing of it may be quite a problem. For example, some roles carry accountability for a number of tasks, each well within the capacity of the person in the role but presenting in total an overall task of programming and progressing that stresses the person considerably.

This often only implicit overall task, of getting the individual tasks completed most advantageously, may be less obvious and less identifiable than the discrete tasks, yet it is the former that indicates the real demands on the person in the role. This overall task is the enveloping one, and it is important that the manager delegating accountability into such a role be aware of whether he is delegating that task also, or retaining it to himself. If he *is* delegating the overall task, then he must be aware of the effect of subsequently changing priorities, or taking a special interest in one of the discrete tasks in the role, in that these actions will tend to destroy the delegation of the overall task.

Another point about certain activities is that they have natural closure-points. For example, a project is finished at an objectively-determined point of completion. Other activities may not have natural closure-points, but if accountability for such an activity is to be delegated properly to another person, then it must be communicated as a task, that is with a closure-point determined in a sense arbitrarily by the manager. It is thus much easier to delegate properly and acceptably in a situation where there are natural closure-points, provided the individuals to whom accountability is delegated have adequate capacity. A temptation, however, is to formulate and delegate tasks solely on the basis of natural closure-points, without taking the capacity of the individual into consideration.

This point may be further complicated in that some work (for example technological development work) may have a natural closure-point beyond the time-scale of the organization that is dealing with it. If the organization is to control this work, then it must be defined in terms of tasks, and closure-points must be determined. This, in its arbitrary or artificial nature, may seriously inhibit some kinds of activity.

The real importance of role is that it links the individual with the organization and the work of the individual with the work of the organization. In short, the situation of 'person in role' has two aspects, the organizational and the personal.

Looking first at the resources in the role, there is an organizational connection between person and resources allocated, that may be called authority, the authority of access to resources. Access to resources is only a part of the situation however, for a person must also have the ability and willingness, the capacity or power to use those resources. These two links between person and resources— the organizational authority of access, and the personal power to use—must reinforce each other rather than conflict, if there is to be an effective situation.

A similar duality links person and the activities in the role. There is the organization link (described here as accountability— what the person is required or allowed to do by the organization), and the purely personal link (described here as responsibility—what the person actually does and how he or she does it). Again, these links should reinforce each other rather than conflict with one another.

Finally, the link with the objectives in the role is not only organizational; because people have personal motives, needs and expectations there is a second and purely personal link which may or may not reinforce the organizational one.

When the person in the role is intelligent, competent, highly trained, or is also perhaps a member of some other organization whose objectives are different from those of the organization in which the role exists, the personal side of the coin is likely to be emphasized, and there may be less ready acceptance of the organizational criteria of performance and standards of work. Where the work itself can be seen to have certain important aspects, or is very closely linked with the work in other roles, the organizational side of the coin is emphasized. Whichever side is emphasized, however, there are always two sides in some kind of interaction.

In summary, the general design points about roles, of every kind, is that the question is always one of boundaries. Figure 6

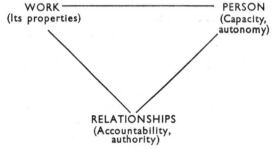

Figure 6—Sources of boundaries

shows this. There are three sources of these boundaries—the work in the role, the person in the role and the interactions between the role and the other roles with which it is related.

The work in the role has certain organizational properties, in the form of objectives, standards, resources needed, programme of activities, and so on, and certain technical properties; these various properties identify boundaries from the work point of the organization's total work, and so it is related with the work in other roles. These relationships also identify boundaries—boundaries between one role and another, which indicate the point at which accountability or authority move from the one role to the other. Then the actual person in the role is the source of boundaries— limits to their capacity in the work.

The work-centred view of boundaries is expressed in terms of accountability and authority, the person-centred view in terms of autonomy, freedom of action, range of discretion.

It is always a mistake, and one that is seen too frequently, to identify roles by titles or functions, by the qualifications of the person in the role, or by grade, or by what the kind of work in the

role appears to be. The danger in all these methods of role identification is that they encourage inferences to be drawn as to the
work-content, authority and accountability, and in particular the
boundaries of the role, which may be totally wrong and misleading.
They do not identify the real content of role, nor the real relationships between the role and others around it. From the point of
view of the effectiveness of the organization, and from that of the
understanding by the person in the role of what it involves, it is
essential that this mistake shall not be made; there is no alternative
to proper specification of role, not for the sake of specification but to
identify those features of role which are the proper determinants of
behaviour and action.

One point connected with this is that a proper statement of
role is an indication of more than the accountability and authority
of the role-occupant. It is also a statement about the accountability
and authority of the person making the statement, defining the role.
Terms of reference, role definitions, task delineations, are always
explicitly or implicitly a statement of the line of demarkation
between the accountability of the person in the role or carrying out
the task and that of the person setting up the role, deciding the
task. They thus form a focus for the relationship between the two
people. It may be that some of the reluctance, met in practice on
occasion, to define roles in proper terms is more to do therefore
with the problems of the person doing the definition than inherently
with the roles themselves.

As an example of the confusion that can arise when role identification is not adequate, I well remember a small engineering firm in
which, because the same kind of engineering skills were needed
in production, in research and development, in technical sales and
in maintenance roles, there was no clarification of accountability
and authority between them, on the basis that the occupants of
these various roles were sensible, mature, reasonable and responsible
engineers. The result certainly did not show that these good human
qualities were sufficient to prevent on the one hand the most serious
conflicts arising on occasion, and on the other certain key tasks from
the point of view of the organization's survival being missed.

The managerial role

A special case of 'role' is the managerial role, and an understanding
of its properties is essential in organization design. A first question

is to do with the concept 'manager'—what does it really amount to? The word 'manager' may be misleading, for in some circumstances it is used only as an indication of the status of the person so described, not as an identification of a particular kind of role. Conversely, in some organizations, although clear managerial roles exist, the term is not used at all, perhaps because it and the related term 'subordinate' are felt to have authoritarian connotations.

There is a particular and recognizable type of role, however, in which there is accountability for work the occupant of the role cannot or will not accomplish single-handed. This kind of role is a key element in organizations and is properly called *managerial*. The term gives no indication as to the level of the role in the organization, nor its importance, nor function, but only to its work content. Since this is of a particular kind—it is not all going to be done by the occupant of the role in person—the implication for authority of access to certain resources must be recognized. The occupant of any role, whatever its nature, has one human resource to control— himself. But what distinguishes the managerial role is the need for authority of access to other human resources; without this, the carrying of accountability for work, some of which is going to be done by other people, is not meaningful. The role-occupant may indeed *feel responsible* for these other people's work, but the design of the *role* is not adequate in this case. What therefore distinguishes the genuine managerial role from the non-managerial is not status, or level, or importance, but the necessity for authority *vis-à-vis* subordinates in the managerial role.

In reality, whatever rationalizations or delusions exist, there is a basic relationship here:—

If real accountability for the work content of a managerial role is to be carried, then the authority in the role must include authority over the other human resources needed for that work, as well as over all the other kinds of resource involved.

If less accountability than this is required, even though perhaps the role is still called 'managerial', then this authority over others is not needed. Conversely, if the required authority over others cannot be established, then the desired accountability cannot exist. There may be degrees of feelings of responsibility between 'full responsibility for the work of others' to 'no responsibility for the work of others' but there are no degrees of accountability; either there is managerial accountability, or there is not. The questions in practice then are ones of how much accountability is desired, how much authority can be established, and these questions cannot be answered in general terms—the particular answers depend on the particular circumstances. But the relationship always stands; there is a minimal level of authority below which the role cannot properly be taken as a genuine 'managerial' one. This is the level below which no accountability can be achieved for the work of others—the person called 'manager' may have a 'watching brief', may keep an eye on the work of the others, may report on their work, or inspect it, but he will not carry accountability for it because he does not have the minimal authority in his role which would achieve this.

This level of authority can now be examined in more detail. If a manager is to be accountable for work which will not be entirely done personally but to some extent by subordinates, then the manager must make at minimum the final decision as to whether his subordinates (as any other resource) are adequate for the work he delegates to them. This means that if accountability is to be achieved, the manager must make the final decisions as to:—

allocation of work to subordinates;
adequacy of subordinates for that work.

People as resources however usually respond sharply to the way in which they are managed, to the manner in which their performance is praised or censured, and to rewards or penalties, and thus the adequacy of subordinates is affected by these factors as well as being a matter of their basic capacity as resources. Thus if the concept of manager is that of carrying accountability for the work of others, the manager must be concerned in these matters, and this applies whether the organization is one in which people are employed for wages or salaries, or is one in which some other form of association is present. The issues are:—

the selection of people for appointment to his subordinate roles;
the removal of inadequate people from his subordinate roles (though not necessarily their removal from the organization);
the kind of work that is assigned to his subordinates and the way it is assigned;
the working conditions under which his subordinates operate;
the subsequent assessment of their performance; and
the sort of praise or criticism, and the rewards, tangible and

intangible, which are offered to them in consequence, and the manner in which they are offered.*

But the manager is not the only person with an interest in these matters. In most organizations, management at higher levels will want (and legitimately so) to retain considerable influence and discretion in all these areas. They too will have a strong interest in the sort of people that are being recruited into the organization and who may well be potential material for higher level roles. They too may have a strong interest in who leaves the manager's team and the mode of their removal. They may wish to specify the type of work that is carried out in each role and much about the way in which that work is carried out. They will normally be considerably involved in the fixing of working conditions—the hours of work, the kind of surroundings, the level of hazard and so on. They will sometimes wish to set down standards, forms and methods of assessment and they will nearly always wish to retain a good deal of control over general and individual levels of reward.

If however the manager is left with the authority to make the final decisions in these issues (and the minimal form, in the last analysis, is that of vetoing other people's decisions) then he is saved from any position in which he is held accountable for achieving certain results in what is an intolerable situation.

The result in terms of managerial authority is that it is inappropriate and ineffective to design a managerial role in which the occupant is expected to be accountable for getting work done through other people, unless the role involves a certain minimal authority *vis-à-vis* those other people. More than this minimal authority may be appropriate in particular situations, but without this minimum the manager is in an intolerable position. To use the term 'managerial' for a role which has less than this minimal authority is to invite confusion, for there is a recognized distinction between the role in which there is accountability for the work of others and the role in which there may be perhaps a 'watching brief' *vis-à-vis* the work of others, but not accountability.

Once the inter-relationship between authority and accountability in the basic managerial role is recognized, then it can be used to illuminate many other aspects and facets of the general managerial requirements in an organization.

For example, I often meet problems of accountability and

* *Organization Analysis* (Newman and Rowbottom, Heinemann 1968).

authority connected with the role of 'supervisor', or connected with the task or responsibility called 'supervision'. Supervision is the task of supervising what others do, whether it is organizational supervision—concerned with the total occupation of role by the person being supervised—or professional or technological supervision—concerned only with those aspects of the person's work. It may be concerned primarily with the results of the activities of the person being supervised, or primarily with the activity itself. At one extreme (sometimes met in industry for example) supervision is the overseeing of the situation to make sure that appropriate results in terms of output are achieved; in other situations (as for example in social services) it takes the form of support and counselling in the way in which the individual deals with his work and its problems. In both instances however the work of the person being supervised is the subject of the relationship.

All this description however does not deal with the problem, which is to do with what supervising really means. Does the role of supervisor require accountability to be carried for the work of those supervised? Or at least for achieving some response in those supervised? Or is it to advise, to counsel, to support, leaving the decision as to whether to use the advice, what response to give, entirely to the person being supervised? These are the kind of questions to be asked and answered if the particular role under scrutiny is to be clarified and effective behaviour in it achieved.

These questions really boil down to two issues. Is the role managerial or is it not? If it is managerial, then what accountability does it require the supervisor to carry *vis-à-vis* the work of those he is supervising? If it is not managerial, then what is the function of the role?

Another aspect of understanding of the managerial role is that of assessing managerial effectiveness. Effectiveness can be assessed only if 'effectiveness at what' is defined and appropriate standards for the particular circumstances determined.

The task of a manager, in any field, is to get things done, the things being of a particular kind—they cannot be done by the manager entirely personally; he gets things done through other people's efforts as well as his own. Tasks have three components—objective, activities and resources. Objective is the result aimed at, and this can be specified in terms of quantity, quality, time and cost standards. Activities should be relevant to objective, and this indicates one criterion of effectiveness. Activities are usually bounded by limits, beyond which the activity is inappropriate, for reasons often connected not with the particular task but with factors from other organizational issues. Resources make tasks feasible, and thus in reality determine the task. The effectiveness of the manager is thus in terms of reaching his objectives, in the light of the resources available to him and within the limits of appropriate activities and use of those resources. In this process, the manager must not only recognize his objectives, but break them down into sub-objectives, to become the objectives for his subordinates. He must delegate tasks, which involves the allocation of resources, to his subordinates, and he must review what is achieved, what is expended, what effect the carrying out of these tasks has had on his resources.

A further issue, which sometimes causes difficulty in the minds of those who are trying to think deeply about the implications of managerial role, follows from the statement that a manager is accountable for the work of his subordinates. The work that his subordinates do involves them in making decisions. Managerial accountability seems to be a desired feature of many organizations, yet it appears at the same time to be in conflict with a basic feature of human behaviour, that people can only really be accountable for the decisions that they themselves make.

How then can a manager be accountable for what someone else does? The answer to this apparent paradox lies in an understanding of what 'work', 'activity', 'what one does' really means and involves.

In order to 'work', or to 'do something', the individual carries out activities which involve the use of resources to achieve some kind of result. The individual's activities are physical and mental, with the mental controlling the physical. The mental activity may be called the 'exercise of discretion'. What a manager does basically is allocate the necessary or available resources into the subordinate's role and indicate the results expected. Thus the manager's mental or discretionary activity is to do with enabling the subordinate to work in a way that is organizationally desirable. The manager does not 'do that work'.

The subordinate is therefore accountable for his own work; the manager's accountability (often described as 'for the subordinate's work') is actually for his own work, which in this context is that of enabling the subordinate to do his work. In reality, the manager manages his subordinates by setting the limits of their freedom of action, within his own limits, set by higher management (Figure 7).

In some organizations there seems to be a different attitude
to questions of control, leadership, clarity of authority and so on
in different units. For example, in units whose work is directly
related to the organization's function there is usually a clear
recognition that effective management is desirable, whatever its
form, whereas in other units, whose work perhaps is regarded as
ancillary, this attitude is sometimes missing. The difference is

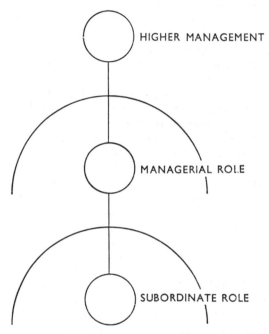

Figure 7—The managerial role

sometimes manifested by the use of the term 'management' in the
first kind of unit and 'administration' in the second. This difference
in attitude is an organizational fault; it is just as important to be
effective and effectively managed in ancillary units as in units
concerned with the major operations of the organization. One of
the reasons for the difference is that sometimes only the management
of what the organization is set up to do is regarded as real management, and all the other units in which people are at work are not
regarded as warranting management.

What is needed is the recognition of 'management of work'—any work—as having certain properties and requirements, and these being clearly established. The particular versions of management, in different units, then can be worked out logically.

The way in which objectives are set for individual managers is worth examining, for it can have a big effect on the manager's attitude of mind and performance.

The structure of the manager's role, and the style within which he himself is managed, should enable him to see what decisions he should take and implement as to the interaction output and capacity objectives at his level. These objectives must be delineated in a way that he can understand, and they must relate to his role, to the things he controls. They must be acceptable to him as well as understood by him, and this means that there must be some provision for dialogue between him and his manager about his objectives. His output objectives should be high enough to warrant attention at his level to them, but not so high as to encourage the jeopardizing of long-term survival. Finally, they must be supported by higher management, who must mean what they say about objectives, and not discard them or allow them to lose status as soon as difficulties arise.

Cross-over manager

A very important but often hidden element of organization structure is the 'cross-over' managerial role. Figure 8 shows this. It has already been mentioned in connection with the problem of a person occupying more than one role, and it appears very frequently in practice in situations where specialists or specialized units relate with general units, and in service-giving/receiving situations. The cross-over role is one which is linked in terms of authority with other roles, not immediately subordinate to it, whose work interacts; the occupant of the cross-over role can mediate between conflicting interests in the subordinate roles if they arise. The need for such cross-over roles is often high, especially in complex organizations, but often they are too far away from the points of conflict to be able to deal with them adequately. It is always helpful in organization design to recognize interactions where conflicts can arise and identify the cross-over managers, establishing them organizationally as near as possible to those interactions. This is an important issue in questions of centralization and decentralization, especially of vital services.

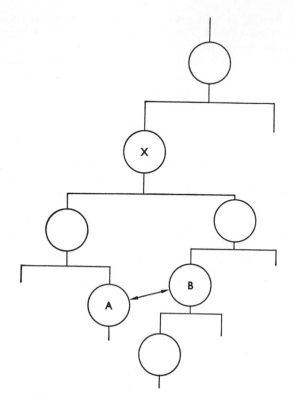

Relationship A— B, Cross—over manager X

Figure 8—The cross-over manager

The executive system

A useful concept is that of the *executive system*.* Every organization contains a set of work-roles, related to one another in some way, and through their occupants the work of the organization is carried out. This set of work-roles may be called the organization's executive system; it includes all the roles, at all levels, and though it is sometimes loosely described as 'the organization' it is really only a part of it, the internal part.

The executive system of roles is usually headed by a chief executive

* This expression was first used in the Glacier Project research.

role (though all sorts of titles are applied to such roles, often with confusion as a result) and the chief executive role may be occupied by an individual or by more than one person. The chief executive in turn is usually accountable for the work of the executive system as a whole to a *directing body*, of which he may or may not be a member. This body is usually formed of or represents those who own the organization or have empowered it to exist or to continue to operate.

This organization—owners, or establishers, directing body, executive system—must possess both internal viability and the maintenance of an adequate relationship with its environment if it is to survive and achieve its objectives.

The directing body

Most organizations have some kind of directing body, whose function is often described as that of 'setting the terms of reference for the executive system'. This body may represent (or indeed in some cases actually be) the owners of the business (as in the case of a Board of Directors) or it may be empowered to manage the organization through say a Chief Officer or Director (as in the case of a Management Committee in a Local Authority).

There is a great deal of confusion and argument in practice about the appropriate role and behaviour of the directing body of an organization, and the subject is one that comes up frequently in questions of organization design. Some of the issues are as follows:—

Very often, members of a directing body occupy other roles. Members of a Board of Directors may be substantial shareholders in the Company; they may be senior managers in the executive system. They may be personally related, and they may have professional relationships or in some cases be members of other bodies or organizations. The problems of occupation of more than one role have already been discussed. If the point about role clarity and differentiation of behaviour is observed however, the problems can be reduced to manageable proportions. It is essential for example that a Company Director who is also a senior manager in the same firm shall not use his status as a Director to distort his authority and accountability as a manager.

Another issue is that of the normally intermittent nature of the directing body's activities compared with those of the executive system. The former meets, probably regularly, but on specific occasions; the other is in operation all the time. This means that the attitude and perception of the directing body, as a whole, is not likely to be identical with that of the members of the executive system, or the chief executive. There is a limit to what direct feelings of responsibility the members of a directing body can develop towards what is going on in the executive system, and a limit to what can be communicated to them about the executive system's experiences. The chief executive in particular needs to recognize that he cannot keep the directing body *au fait* with all that is going on in the executive system all the time, and the directing body needs to understand why this is so. It also follows that, because the executive system is continuously involved with its activities and the directing body is only intermittently involved, the rate of development of experience, knowledge and attitude is likely to be higher in the former, and thus the communications and general relationship between them is likely to change with time. Where the relationship between directing body and executive system is a good one, it is usual to find that through time it develops into one to do more with basic resources and mutual trust than with actual operations, except in review.

A point to remember about directing bodies is that even if they represent the 'owners of the business' they do not necessarily represent the real owners of all the resources that are involved in the operations of the organization. For example, a Board of Directors may perhaps represent the shareholders of the Company, or a Management Committee may represent the suppliers of the financial resource to a Local Authority service, but in neither case do they automatically represent the owners of the human resource in the organization, for this resource is owned by the individuals in whom it exists. It is essential in organization design therefore that the real limitations to what the directing body can represent or control are identified.

A situation that is sometimes met, particularly in large organizations, is where the directing body itself in reality is subordinate to some other body or person. For example, one member of the directing body (usually the Chairman) may be the owner of the assets of the organization; in this case, the directing body can only act as such within the limits of acquiescence of that member. If the directing body is to be effective as such in this kind of situation, the limits of its actions must be consistent; the Chairman should not expect it to operate as a genuine directing body on some occasions and abrogate its function on others.

Another case is when the directing body is subordinate to a higher-level directing body. This occurs for example when the directing body is the Board of Directors of a subsidiary company in a large industrial firm. The real role of the directing body in this situation needs to be understood, in terms of authority and accountability, by reference to the roles of the superior directing body and its chief executive, and the chief executive of the subordinate organization. Quite often, the chief executive of the subordinate organization has as his manager not his subsidiary Board of Directors but the chief executive of the superior organization. If this is the case, then the directing body of the subordinate organization is more of an advising group than a genuine directing body. One of the results of mergers and takeovers that is sometimes not understood at the time and thus causes difficulties and conflict is that a genuine directing body may become in reality only an advising body after the takeover, even though its designation, status and membership may remain unchanged.

So far as function is concerned, setting the terms of reference for the executive system means defining its limits of autonomy; this is often done through the definition of the role of the chief executive. As yet, however, there is little available data from systematic investigation of what directing bodies actually do, and there is a great deal of questioning at present, especially in terms of the functions of Boards of Directors, about such things as social responsibilities and the control of management style. It has been suggested* that the directing body has five basic functions, to do with:—

strategic planning;
policy making;
organization and management development;
monitoring operations and performance against main objectives;
making key corporate decisions.

Fundamentally, the directing body must be concerned with the identification of the organization's objectives (either positively or by agreeing to the proposals of the chief executive), with the supply of resources to the organization, at the time and into the future, with the organization's relationships with its environment, and with the performance of the executive system in that light.

* British Institute of Management Conference, 1971 (Hugh Parker), *The Arts of Top Management* (Hugh Parker, McGraw-Hill 1970).

E

Other role relationships

The feature 'role' and its particular version 'managerial role' are the key design factors in any executive system, however it is structured in the broad sense. To the extent that different roles carry accountability for different work, different tasks, then various kinds of role relationships will occur. The manager/subordinate relationship has already been discussed, developing as a result of a particular kind of accountability—accountability for a subordinate's work. There are various other possible relationships however, including two main kinds—collateral and staff.

*Collateral relationships**

It may be a pity to use a special term 'collateral' when a perfectly appropriate term 'colleague' exists, but I am doing so because the latter is often used in a very general sense indeed, to include everyone in a general situation, or perhaps at a similar level. I am using the word 'collateral' to describe a particular relationship between roles whose work content directly interacts, whose occupants therefore make decisions and carry out tasks which affect each other's accountability. One is dependent to some extent on the other, yet neither has authority over the other. This kind of relationship often exists for example between production roles and sales roles in industrial firms, or between the roles of different professionals concerned with the same client, in organizations offering multi-professional services.

What is important in designing this kind of relationship is that the boundaries of accountability and authority shall be clear. When there is no problem in the relationship, it is tempting to think that clarity of boundary is unnecessary; when problems occur, however, the relationship is likely to be inherently one of conflict, and it is much better to have the boundaries clarified at an easier time than wait until things are difficult. If the interacting accountabilities in the two roles cannot be reconciled, then the boundaries of the roles must be changed, and this is where the 'cross-over manager' comes into focus again, because the boundaries of one of the individual roles cannot be changed effectively without changing those of the other role. Thus the authority to make this kind of change is in the

* This expression was first used in this context in the Glacier Project research.

role of the manager who is concerned with both the roles in question. Again, there can be a serious problem if this cross-over manager role is too far away.

Service relationships

A particular case of collateral relationship is that of service-giving/service-receiving, and it is one that sometimes is not given as much attention in the design sense as it warrants. The essential feature of a true service-giving role is that the accountability is for giving the service as a response to requests; the service-giver cannot impress the service on those who use it. Sometimes roles are erroneously described as service-giving when in fact they have the authority to insist on the service being used; these are a kind of 'staff' role, and should always be distinguished from service-giving roles.

The supplying of services by one unit or one manager to another is always potentially a situation of difficulty, however good the relationships, because the units have different accountabilities; their interests and objectives are different. Contentious issues must be taken to the cross-over point, and for this, the cross-over manager must be identified, must not be too far away, must be willing to act, and above all must recognize the recourse to the cross-over point as organizationally necessary and not a 'confession of failure'.

The issues that are likely to be contentious in a service-giving/service-receiving relationship are the questions of priority of access to the service and of the quality of the service. As a general approach, the service-receiver should be accountable for specifying what service is required, the service-giver for the quality and for deciding the priorities of demands for the service, both within set down limits of freedom, or policy regulating the service. The service-giver must give the service if within the limits of his role and his resources; discretion as to whether or not to offer the service is not normally his.

As far as possible, services that are an essential part of the resources that a manager must have should not be positioned under the control of a colleague. This raises of course the whole question of centralization of services; there is usually a sound and quantifiable economic argument for centralization, but it is essential that this be balanced by an attempt to identify the effect on availability, from the user's point of view, and above all, on the user's accountability.

Faulty situations I have seen have been where people have given services which were not within their roles to give; they liked giving them, or they gave them 'for the good of the organization', or as a *quid pro quo*, or for status reasons. Occasionally I have heard of people being criticized for giving services which they were in fact required to give—but their manager had forgotten about them.

Obviously there are many design elements in all this, and they are worth considering sharply; access to services is a way of augmenting resources, but if not adequately designed and controlled it can run away and become a very high hidden expense. The supply of services is never really open-ended, but the demand for them tends to rise rapidly as their provision is extended, because increased availability tends to mean that they are used in situations of decreasing importance. Limits should therefore be set to the availability of services, to ensure that they are only used in justifiable circumstances. It is often helpful to recognize that the use of a service is equivalent to spending money. Every requisition therefore is a commitment to expense, and one way to achieve a businesslike approach to the use of services is to think of such use as if it were a call on an external contractor. There should be clear limits to the availability and quality of service; without these, the accountability of the user of the service for what use is made of it may be lost.

One point connected with the provision of services within an organization, which sometimes has big design implications, is the way in which decisions are made as to where the service resources should be provided and controlled. Should typing services for example be allocated out to the units needing them, or should they be pooled as a central service? There are arguments on both sides, but it is essential not to make the mistake of letting the design of the services (in the organizational sense) be decided only by the quantitative advantages of centralization or pooling, in the absence of recognition of the possible effects on availability. The mistake is that when efficiency or cost-effectiveness analyses are made, the value of availability is not adequately included because it cannot be quantified. As a result, undue weight may be given to the efficiency of the service, and the effectiveness of the relationship between the service and those who need it (which is the proper efficiency to achieve) is missed. A way to deal with this is to identify the effect of non-availability on those who need the service; this often can be quantified.

Another aspect of availability is its effect on the motivation of the service-giver. The state of availability, like that of the bridesmaid, may become intolerable if it goes on too long without being used. There is a limit therefore to availability in practice, from the point of view of the service-giver, and a limit usually to lack of availability, from the point of view of the service-requirer. It is helpful to identify these limits if possible, since the region between them is that of the reasonable working relationship, and on this basis the cost-analysis or efficiency should be assessed.

Staff relationships

A staff relationship is one in which there is a difference in authority between the two roles, unlike the collateral relationship, but this difference does not extend to one of managerial authority. The staff relationship therefore falls between the manager/subordinate and the collateral. This kind of relationship occurs where it is desirable that instructions be given by people who are not managerially accountable for the work of those whom the instructions affect. The occupant of the staff role is very often a specialist in a particular field, and the object of the staff relationship is that he shall have more than a service-giving effect, he shall influence in a positive way in terms of his own specialism the work of others in the executive system. Very often, of course, the service-giving feature is also present; a personnel officer in an industrial organization may be in a staff role in the sense that he gives instructions to people who are not his subordinates, these instructions being to do with the implementation of the organization's personnel policy, and he may also offer to those same people the service of advice in the personnel problems with which they have to deal. At the same time of course he may well be in a managerial role, having his own subordinates in his own specialism to manage. Obviously there is plenty of scope for confusion and distortion of authority if these various relationships are not clearly understood and differentiated.*

The main points about a staff role are that the authority over others is in a defined area or field only, and it must not encroach into the minimal authority of those others' managers. The occupant of a staff role is not accountable for the work of those to whom he gives instructions; he is accountable for the quality of those instructions, and the relationship is basically regulated by explicit or

* See for example *Organization Analysis* (Newman and Rowbottom, Heinemann 1968).

implicit policies which can requisitely only be established by the cross-over manager or higher authority.

Deputies and assistants

There are many other role titles in some organizations. Deputy, Assistant, Assistant to, Personal Assistant are some of them, and they sometimes cause a great deal of confusion. There seem to be two main sources of this confusion. One has already been mentioned —the role title is taken to indicate the content of the role, and different people interpret it in different ways. The other is the confusion between these titles as indicative of the role, and the titles as significant in a grading or status system. For example, the title 'deputy' sometimes indicates that the person involved has a certain status or perhaps is at a certain grade of salary, and has nothing to do with their role; they have no more authority than others without that particular title. I have even met situations where although there is someone called 'deputy' in a unit, the person who deputizes for the manager in the manager's absence is someone else, without the title 'deputy'. There is often a lot of argument about the difference between 'assistant' and 'assistant to'. What matters however is the recognition that these terms can all be used to mean what the user wants to mean—they have no general discrete significance. In organization design, therefore, roles with these titles must be identifiable in terms of authority and accountability, there is no other way to achieve clarity.

Procedures and policies

Any feature within an organization, whether or not it appears to be anything to do with the organization's structure, that delineates or limits the freedom of people in the organization to act as they decide, to use discretion, to exercise authority or carry accountability, has structural and therefore design implications. Many of the problems I meet in organizations are not basically due to structural issues directly, but result from design changes that have not been thought through fully in terms of other features.

Laid-down procedures for example nearly always affect people's freedom of action, in the situational or process sense, sometimes both. All procedures contain potential structural implications and this must always be remembered when structure or procedures are changed. Any procedure that limits the freedom of an individual to act as he desires, or which sets boundaries in time to that freedom of action, or that regulates the relationship between the occupants of different roles in the organization, has very clear design constraints in it.

Similarly, the policies that have been established and are operated in an organization or part of one often have powerful design implications. Policies often indicate priorities, or how things are to be done in certain circumstances, or the bases of decisions that must be taken. They always indicate boundaries of autonomy if they are effectively formulated, and one way in which an organization design degenerates in effectiveness or credibility is that policies are developed, or changes made in organization structure, without considering the relationship between policies and structure. Before these implications can be dealt with however it is necessary to recognize that the term 'policy' can stand for more than one kind of thing.

For example, many organizations tell me that they have a Personnel Policy, or a Training Policy, or Machinery Maintenance Policy. What I find on examination of these policies is two different kinds of statement. One kind is to do with the way the unit or department concerned is to operate; the Personnel Policy to take one example of this kind identifies what the tasks are of the Personnel Department of the organization concerned, how it will operate, what its role is. The other kind is to do with the relationships between the unit concerned and the other units within the organization with which it interacts; in this kind of case the Personnel Policy identifies the boundaries of authority and accountability between the Personnel Department and the units with which it relates, and establishes the conditions for intervention, one way or the other. Both these kinds of policy have design implications, one within the unit or function concerned, the other in terms of the interactions between that unit and those with which it relates, and both are important. Sometimes only the first kind is established explicitly, and the second is informal and thus subject to all kinds of distortions and pressures.

The most effective practical way to ensure that the design implications of policies are understood is to test them out against difficult decisions that need to be made. This is for the obvious reason, if one thinks about it, that policies are of little consequence when they do not need to be invoked, but when difficult decisions are to be made the policy if meaningful at all will have something to say about the accountability and authority for those decisions. Again, the main point to recognize is that policies, in the situational sense, or the process sense, or both, regulate the interactions between departments and between roles, set boundaries of freedom of action into the future, aim at preventing inconsistencies, and so on, and all these functions demonstrate aspects of structure.

I.5 The organization's environment

No real organization, whatever its nature, exists in a void. The people in some organizations sometimes behave as though this were not so; they act as if the organization had no need to relate with anything outside itself, and even get away with this occasionally, for a while. But not for long, for the organization's effectiveness, and indeed its survival, depends on how it relates with the context or environment within which it exists, as well as on its internal effectiveness, and this is so, whether or not the main purpose of the organization requires this relationship with its environment to be achieved in a positive way.

The organization's environment is not normally a simple field within which the organization exists, but a complex set of features that includes the suppliers of the resources that the organization needs, the recipients of the goods or services that the organization supplies and the general scene (economic, political, social, legal, fiscal, cultural, physical) in which the organization operates. In addition, if the organization under consideration is part of a larger organization, then this larger or surrounding organization is likely to be a very significant part of its environment.

Each feature of the environment presents a set of determinants and constraints to the existence and the operations of the organization, and if the organization is to remain effective these determinants and constraints must be identified and dealt with effectively. This means that the changes in them must be responded to as well as their presence recognized.

To the extent that the environment has an active relationship with the organization, it may be seen as a complex system of power groups, these being the various groups that have an interest in the operations of the organization and the power to modify or to prevent those operations. For example, in the case of a typical commercial organization, one power group is the shareholders, the owners of the financial assets. Another is that of the suppliers of materials and services needed by the organization. A third is that of the human beings who are the employees of the organization— this group is often organized in the form of trade unions, staff associations, etc. Others are the other suppliers of finance, trade associations, the general public, local and central government. In each case, the group has some interest in the operations of the organization, and has some measure of power to affect those operations if it chooses to use it.

In this sense, the organization may be likened to an organism which needs to come to terms, in a dynamic way, with the various significant elements of its environment in order to survive and go on moving towards its own objectives. This means that it must recognize them, see how they change, decide which are the most important and how this changes, and organize internally to relate with them.

Relationship analysis

An organization therefore must relate effectively with the features of its environment, and the development of the structure to enable this set of effective relationships to be achieved is a major part of organization design. A very useful tool for the design of any relationship is 'relationship analysis', and it is particularly illuminating in this context. It shows what needs to be designed, and achieved, if the relationships between the organization and its environment are to be effective as a result of positive action rather than by accident. This is not to deny that some organizations are very successful in their relationships with their environment, without any of this analytical thinking, but to indicate that conscious organization design requires it. Furthermore, an examination of successful organizations shows sharply that by one means or another, the following questions have been answered:—

> What are the entities in the relationship, and how are they changing or how should they change?
> What are the contents of the transaction in the relationship, and how are they changing or how should they change?
> What are the processes of achieving the transaction, and how are they changing or how should they change?

These questions must be answered, the way the answers change through time and changing circumstances must be recognized, and the answers must be acted upon, if the relationship is to be designed as an effective one. It was said recently that 'the best organizations, whatever their *raison d'être,* change in anticipation of changes in their surroundings, not as a delayed reaction'. Relationship analysis is a tool that enables this to be achieved, for each of the significant features in the organization's environment. It is shown graphically in Figure 9.

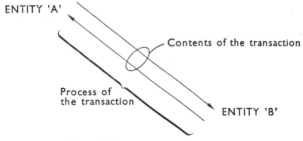

Figure 9—Relationship analysis

There are some extremely important general results of using relationship analysis to see what needs to be designed in the interaction between an organization and its environment. In order to answer the first question, it must be possible not only to identify the environmental features of significance, but also to identify what the organization itself—the other entity in the relationship—is trying to be. How these entities are changing or should change must also be identified. Suppose we are dealing with a typical commercial firm, and the relationship under consideration is that with the shareholders, or perhaps that with the market, then data about who the shareholders are (pretty obvious) and how their make-up is changing (not perhaps quite so obvious) and what the organization is trying to be *vis-à-vis* the shareholders (often not obvious at all) are essential if that relationship is to be designed and developed. Similarly, who the market is, how the market is changing, how the organization wants it to change (especially in terms of the potential market) and what the organization is trying to be *vis-à-vis* the market are all necessary subjects of exploration for effective design, and techniques such as market research and those to do with establishing the image of the firm can now be seen in context.

In terms of the second broad question, issues such as what the shareholders supply to the firm, what they get back, how this content is changing, or what the market gets from the firm, what it pays in return, and how these are changing or should change, arise. These lead to the delineation of tasks within the organization to do with financial transactions with shareholders (and also, if the firm is perceptive, transactions of a psychological content, of confidence, information, and so on) or the production of goods or services on the one hand, the establishment of prices for them on the other, and research and development concerned with changes needed in them.

Finally, as a result of the third broad question, procedures for selling shares, for paying dividends and so on, or methods of supplying goods to the market (sales) and collecting payment for them are identified as needing designing.

PART II

Organization design

II.1 General considerations

In the Introduction I said that organization design was the design of the organization structure, using the term 'structure' in its widest sense. Before going into the question of organization design at large, it is essential to be clear about what this structure is, and the best way to do this is to recognize what organization structure is for. The function of structure in any kind of body or entity is to hold the thing together, to give it form rather than randomness, to give it consistency and stability, to relate its part one to another, to delineate its operations. This is very much so in the case of organization structure. In essence, therefore, organization structure delineates and regulates in a consistent way the work, the actions and the behaviour of the people in the organization, in their relationships with each other, with the organization's environment and above all with the organization's objectives. Any feature that does this delineating or regulating is thus structural or has structural implications, and it is essential for effective design that all such features are identified and taken into consideration. For example, however the overt aspects of an organization's structure are designed, if there are consistent and strongly established patterns of behaviour in the situation then these also will act as structural features, and they may or may not reinforce or relate with the overt structure. If they conflict with it, then the design of the overt structure will not be effective. In addition, such things as wages and salary policies, or ways of assessing people's performance and value to the organization have structural implications because they affect the behaviour of people in a consistent way. Overt structural design must therefore take them also into consideration.

There seem to be three basic features of organization that lead to the need for structure. One is the organization's work, in the 'situational' sense of objectives and their delegation, desired activities, and resources and their allocation. This feature leads to the concepts of work-role and role structure. Another is the organization's work in the 'process' sense of decisions being made, resources used, activities carried out, and this leads to the concepts of role and role-relationships in the dynamic sense. The third is to do with the behaviour of people in the organization, in their relationships with one another; this leads to some consistency of expectation, and thus to structure. In practice, the structural implications of these three features are inter-related, but they are not necessarily mutually compatible or reinforcing, and one of the arts of organization design is in evolving the structure of the organization so as to achieve as much reinforcement as possible between these features.

It is important to recognize that although the first two features are the ones that are to do with the organization's work, and the third is not, nevertheless it is the third that finally determines the real structure of relationships in practice. If however the first two are inadequate, inappropriate behaviour may develop as a consequence, and the effect of this may be a serious constraint on the situation even after adequate work structure has been re-established. Similarly, in a situation of change, behaviour structure which in the past has been entirely appropriate may persist long after the work and its process and their appropriate structure have been changed.

In short, any organization involves sets of relationships, between people, between roles, between units, whether or not these relationships are recognized formally. To the extent that there is some consistency or an expectation of more than randomness in a relationship then there is 'structure' in that relationship, and this feature of relationships is a basic source of organization structure.

The main case for formalizing organization structure to some extent is that this reveals the features of the relationships that are desired, and enables consistency to be more readily and more objectively achieved. If the structure is completely formalized however, no route will be left by which intolerable aspects of the organizational situation, if they develop, may be escaped. It certainly appears in practice that this sometimes puts a limit to the extent to which formal structure, or the exposure it produces, can be effective. If this limit is exceeded, in an attempt perhaps to formalize the structure completely, it is likely that a randomness or a different set of real features of relationships will develop, whereas below that limit the formalization may have reinforced what is desired.

To many people, emotionally, the ideal form of organization

structure would be the fully 'informal' one—that in which everyone knew and accepted their roles and fitted in to the organization without having to be directed, and without formal structure or role specification. This situation would more accurately be described as a 'self-induced' organizational situation rather than an 'externally-induced' one. For it to be possible, and effective, what kind of people would the members of the organization need to be?

The criteria would be:—

No personal power-seeking.

No misconception as to task, and as to task relevance to organization's objectives.

No incompatibilities of personality or between personality and relevant work.

Since these criteria are never fully met in a real situation, then some degree of formal organization is needed, as a framework to ensure that the situation of not quite meeting these criteria is not self-degenerating or unacceptably damaging to the organization's work and health.

It is necessary (if a move towards the ideal is to be achieved) that the elements of formal organization are continually reviewed in order to keep them appropriate to the changing work situation and the changing human situation. As people become more adequate in their jobs, and more mature in their personal relationships—developed as a result of their job relationships—then the degree of formal organization can and should be reviewed and relaxed.

There is often a link between the extent of formalization of structure and the size of the organization, in that as size or complexity increases, there is almost inevitably an increase in formalized procedures, rules and regulations, roles and role-structure, because more relationships need to be clarified and regulated. This may have paradoxical effects. If the increase in formalization is based on real requirements, then it results in increased exposure of what is required, what is supposed to happen, what relationships are requisite, and this leaves less room for speciousness, 'politics', and so on, and would appear therefore to improve the organization. Because it leaves less room for individual autonomy, less room for manoeuvre, however, often the reverse happens, and the formal structure and procedures fall into some disrepute, with the real relationships becoming increasingly based on 'politics' rather than 'work'. Good organization design recognizes these tendencies and keeps the situation under constant review.

Broad design

If the design of an organization is to be an effective one, then it must enable the effective work of the organization to be identified, communicated, perceived and carried out at all levels. This means, broadly, that there are two main aspects of design—the general structure and orientation of the organization as a whole, and the specific roles and relationships within it. These aspects of the design must be thought through—there is no alternative—with competent knowledge of the determinants and constraints in the situation.

Unfortunately, sometimes in place of such analytically-based thinking, popular 'slogans' are the starting point for design. Their danger is that they probably contain an element of good sense, but as bases of design they are wrong. Examples of such slogans are 'decentralization is a good thing', 'we must be market-oriented', 'services must be centralized to be economically effective'; the truths in these slogans must be related to the particular circumstances involved before they are taken as valid in other circumstances.

Before any questions of design at large are dealt with however, there is a paramount issue to be tackled, that of the organization's objectives. The design of an organization depends on the objectives of the organization and their implications for action. The organization must be designed for what it is *for*, and what it is for must therefore be identified first.

The main practical issues in an organization design are thus:—

the recognition of the organization's objectives;
the identification of the way or ways in which the organization is trying to achieve its objectives; the general structure and orientation of the organization;
the specific roles and relationships within it.

Enough has been said earlier to show that the factors that affect these issues are:—

the desired relationships between the organization and its environment;

the desired relationships inside the organization in a situational sense;

the desired relationships inside the organization in a process sense.

These sets interact with each other; they can be separated analytically but in practice their interaction is close and iterative. Each set involves interactions of its own, and the result of organization design is thus always a compromise or set of compromises. There is no such thing as a right or perfect design. There is a right starting point for design however, and this is the question of the objectives of the organization.

It is a pity that sometimes the issues involved in organization design are falsely or too extremely polarized, leading to swings of fashion or, at least, misconceptions that can only inhibit the development of better organizations. An example of this was given some time ago in a symposium on the relationship between creativity and organizational structure. In this symposium there was almost unanimous agreement on the need for 'organic as opposed to hierarchical structure if creativity were to be fostered'. Another is in the comment in an address to social workers that 'institutions with a democratic structure were slower than competitive-based organizations to use new techniques and methods of work'.

The first of these statements is probably true, as far as it goes, but it does not go far enough. Creativity for creativity's sake is not a feature of many real organizations. Creativity that is then implemented in design, in development, in new products and services, new ways of doing things, is a much more realistic thing, and if we accept this then we must also recognize that the implementation of creative thought and art may well need some kind of hierarchical structure in order to make it feasible and effective.

In the second statement, the question of whether quicker introduction of new techniques is necessarily a good thing is being begged, as is the question of whether institutions can decide not to have a 'democratic structure' anyway, or whether that decision is a result of the kind of people in the institution.

F

II.2 The organization's objectives and tasks

In considering the objectives of any organization, in any field, an immediate and fundamental point must be faced. Whatever terms are used, and however the people involved think and communicate about organizational objectives, it is axiomatic that in order for the organization's objectives to be acted upon, the organization must be capable of operating, of action; it must survive in an effective state. Conversely, in order to survive, to be capable of action, the organization's objectives must be such as to enable that survival to continue.

The real organization then has two basic objectives—one is what it is for, the other is to achieve what enables it to continue. One may be regarded as objective, the other prerequisite, or constraint. But what is essential is that neither shall in general be regarded as more important, more prime, than the other. There may be points in time when attention to one is more necessary or more urgent than attention to the other, but the status of these two basic objectives is equal; one depends on the other. I prefer to call them both objectives, for two reasons. One is to ensure that their relative status is not distorted by the terms used for them. The other is that to different units or functions within the organization they each may in fact be the source, the objective, of specific tasks.

One, what the organization is for, might be called the *output* objective; the other, which is to do with the organization's continuing ability to meet the output objective, might be called the *capacity* objective. Both need positive action to be taken, organization structures developed, if they are to be met effectively, but fundamentally the interaction between them—in sharp terms the determination of how much effort is to be put into output and how much into survival—is a matter of judgment, and should change as circumstances change. If this kind of judgment is not made, and its organizational implications met, then no amount of subsequent organizational design, clarification of objectives, and so on, will be adequate—there is something vital missing.

Whatever the intention of the organization, whatever its purpose, if it is to survive and be effective it must recognize these two primary objectives. The organization must do something about them, and they are both primary in the sense that whatever other objectives and constraints exist, these two must be established and their interaction understood. They are in competition for attention.

The effective organization then is one which identifies its appropriate objectives, achieves them and goes on achieving them. Of course, it is a tempting suggestion but a dangerous one in practice that the organization should identify its single 'primary objective', and then everything else would fall into place as a matter of logical analysis. Unfortunately, if this approach is pursued, the ensuing description of objective is inevitably one that begs the questions it is intended to answer—how to survive effectively, how to go on being successful, how to go on relating with the environment—and it invites abdication from the vitally important decision as to the distribution of effort between output and facilities objectives.

The output objective leads to tasks to do with the organization's output, results, positive actions, and so on, and the capacity objective leads to tasks concerned with the obtaining, conservation and development of facilities and resources. It is perhaps significant to see that the presence of these two objectives is now being recognized nationally, in the interaction between the desire for further improvement in the gross national product, or standard of living, and the desire for conservation of the environment, or improvement in the quality of life. Attention to one of these is in competition with attention to the other. One is a constraint on the other. Both are important for effective survival.

Effective organization design has as its precursor the identification of these two objectives and what they imply in the specific organization concerned, and the competition between them for attention, for resources, recognized and dealt with. Dealing with it is a matter of judgment rather than logic alone—there is no right balance between them—and this means that it is a difficult and to some extent an emotional matter, dependent on the values people hold and their views of the future. If this judgment is not exercised, and the balance of tasks that should follow therefore not established, no subsequent organization design will be fully effective. A serious fault in some organizations is that the desired balance of effort is not established at the top but is differentially determined by various managers or units, from their own point of view and the properties of their own function. This will always lead to arguments and recriminations about performance and effectiveness, to bias in judgment about priorities and to loss of real organizational control.

Some organizations superficially appear to be in a special category in this respect. These are organizations whose survival is 'artificially determined'—it does not appear to depend on their own efforts or effectiveness. An example may be a civil service organization, which looks as though it will continue to survive whatever the level and standards of its performance, because the determinant of survival is extra-organizational. In fact, the same real considerations apply to the factors leading to *effective* survival, but there is an escape available to top management in such a situation from the difficult and emotional decision as to the distribution of attention between the two objectives. Thus it is likely to be more difficult to be effective in this crucial aspect of distribution of effort in such an organization than in the situation where the organization's survival depends on its own efforts alone. It follows therefore that in such a situation the top management should be even clearer about the two objectives and their implications and strong enough to make the required decisions, if their organization is to be an effective one.

This whole question of objectives causes a great deal of confusion and hence basic inadequacy of organization design in practice. I find that the most helpful way to identify objectives and their implications, leading on to the basis for organization design, is to see that whatever the underlying *raison d'être* of the organization, the actions it must take are related to the output and capacity objectives. These must be recognized, their required interaction decided, and then the task objectives that follow can be defined, using an understanding of the different concepts of objective to identify the organizational consequences. Figure 10 shows this process graphically.

Finally, it is necessary to look at the question of organizational objectives in process terms. Two main points are then exposed. First, organizations exist in environments—physical, economic, social, cultural—which directly or indirectly affect their objectives, either as determinants or constraints. The way in which an organization, through its executive system, positively attempts to achieve its objectives thus requires it to maintain effective relationships with the significant parts of its environment, and these relationships then supply it with the resources and facilities that enable it to continue.

Second, the processes whereby objectives are formulated, or indeed any decisions are made, are not the same as the process whereby objectives are met, or decisions are implemented. In formulating and deciding objectives there are many possible

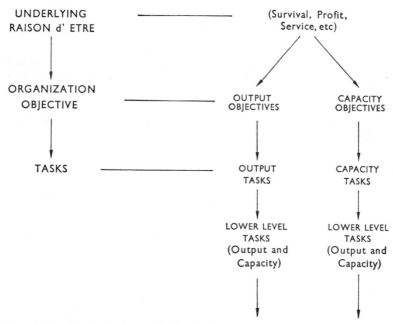

Figure 10—The basis of organization design

processes, ranging from the unilateral dictatorial to the egalitarian democratic; what is appropriate and effective depends on many factors. The process for meeting objectives on the other hand is one which involves the identification, development and use of resources and the carrying out of relevant activities. This process in any form of organization appears to involve a hierarchical structure of some sort, whatever the objectives or ways of determining those objectives, whether its structure is formal or informal, explicit or implicit, and whether the style of behaviour in the structure is authoritarian or permissive.

The process of meeting objectives of course is not unconnected with the process for deciding objectives. To the extent that people in an organization have power to affect or prevent the organization's viability or continuing operation, then their understanding and acceptance of the objectives of the organization has a significant effect on their activities. To achieve this understanding and acceptance of organization objectives, it may be necessary that they should effectively be involved in the process for determining those objectives.

This whole question of what the objectives of the organization should be often causes a great deal of confusion in practice. I think that the confusion occurs largely because several different questions or issues are mixed up together. It is a frequent experience of mine to sit with a group of people discussing the objectives of their organization, and after sifting through the problem with them find that there are really four separate issues involved. One is that of the form of objective—as discussed earlier, there is more than one form, and each has different organizational and managerial implications. Connected with this issue is the need in practice to identify task objectives. A second is the question of multiplicity of the organization's objectives, especially when it is understood that what are felt to be constraints rather than objectives may well be recognized as objectives when considered from a different viewpoint. A third is the question of the attitude of the people involved to their organization's objectives, and last but by no means least in confusing effect is the question of terminology. Only when these different issues have been seen can an effective way of dealing with them be discussed and evolved.

Objectives and change

Another point about an organization's objectives is that they have originally been the basis of the genesis of the organization. Organizations form or are set up as a result of recognition of objectives or needs that cannot be reached or met as a result of the efforts of individuals in isolation. For example, a group of people may decide that they could better exploit their own knowledge or develop their own possessions or protect their own interests if they come together and become organized. A government may recognize a social need and set up an organization to deal with it. A group of potential shareholders may subscribe to a company and set up an organization to achieve for them a profit on their investment, and so on. Whatever the form of organization or the method of its formation, and whatever kinds of activity go on in it, it results from an objective or objectives of a particular kind—they cannot be reached or satisfied by individuals in isolation. The structure of the organization, the activities carried out in it, the resources employed and the behaviour and culture of the people in it should all be consequential upon the objectives (as well as being affected by the environment—physical, social, economic, political and so on—within which the organization exists). Once formed, these features of structure, activities, relationships and so on develop and become in a sense 'the organization'.

However, as organizations change, grow or become more complex, and particularly if their objectives change, these features may for a time become further and further separated from or less and less effectively relevant to the objectives which should be their basis. The reason for this is two-fold. In the first place, as mentioned earlier, these features are all affected by the environment of the organization, and this puts a constraint on the rate at which they can change or be changed. In the second place, these features, as 'the organization', have a stability and coherence of their own, not dependent on objectives but as a result of the way they interact and relate together. This stability is an important and necessary feature of real organizations, for without the structure and relationships that form it the achievement of ordered and effective means towards the objectives is not likely. Furthermore, some structured stability (formal or informal) appears to be desired by most people in organizations as a basis of their activities.

This organizational stability from one point of view therefore is necessary and helpful; from another point of view, that of change or flexibility, it is a constraint. This is one of the basic dilemmas of organization, between stability and flexibility. Both are needed in reality, and the key to each is structure. The ideal situation is that in which structure, in all its aspects, remains relevant to objectives as they change, and yet gives the necessary stability and effectiveness to the organization and is appropriate in terms of the environment within which the organization exists. In practice, what is always seen is some compromise or, in some instances, gross discontinuity between the implications of objectives, of environmental factors and of the internal organizational factors. For example, in some organizations, objectives have changed a great deal, and more quickly than the organization structure has been changed to suit. Sometimes this results in almost total inadequacy or failure to achieve new objectives, because the existing structure, perhaps strongly reinforced by environmental factors, continues to 'force activities into its own mould', so that the only effective activities are not relevant to the new objectives. In other instances, because of the way in which change has been instituted, the 'organization attitude' is one of reaction to change rather than of positive association with it, so that even if appropriate structural re-organization has been carried out—on paper—the real relationships do not change. On the other hand, in one situation known to me a sharp conflict has built up between the informal structure, which, reinforced by environmental factors, has developed in line with new objectives because they are approved of by people in the organization, and the formal structure which has not changed. This is a very sad state of affairs, where the formal structure which should enable and encourage the carrying out of relevant activities in fact is inhibiting them, and the particular case in mind shows the even sadder effect that the more responsibly-minded people are the most damaged by it, since they see the need to support the formal organization and for loyalty to their seniors who represent it, yet cannot accept it as anything but damaging to their work and to what they believe is the desired objective and spirit.

Another situation is where the organization has changed to become more relevant to changing objectives, but this has put it and individuals within it into a state of increasing stress in relationship with the environment. This has happened for example in developing countries where the rate of social/cultural change in industrial organizations may be very much higher than that in general. It has also occurred in developed countries where for instance an organization may have achieved internal relationship with its employees which was relevant to its objectives and acceptable to them, but caused difficulties with an external factor such as a Trade Union.

On occasion, this sort of situation arises when a new organization is set up, or a new part of an existing organization is developed. Because it is considered to be in a particular field, say industrial, or educational, or civil service, or social service, it is organized in the way of that field in general, or as organizations in that field are supposed to be. This can result in a discontinuity *ab initio* between the implications of objectives and the organization structure; the structure often rapidly develops a stability and coherence of its own which is then very difficult to change. This can happen particularly when the organizational field to which this new organization or new part is considered to belong is one having long traditions, strong culture or possibly a sense of being threatened by the development of the new organization. There are many examples of this kind of problem, ranging from attempts by industrial organizations to diversify, where a new product or technology fails to be effective because it is forced into an existing structure and style that may be very effective for other activities but not for this one, to attempts in Government organizations to do new kinds of work, or reflect new social attitudes and expectations but using the same structure and style that is associated automatically with the generic 'State organization' or 'Civil Service'.

Without suggesting that Government or State organizations are the only ones prone to problems of dissociation between objectives and structure, there are two further features of some organizations that are worth considering in this context, since they may exacerbate the problems. One is that the objective of some such organizations in whole or in part is to do with 'preserving the *status quo*', perhaps conserving the stability and security of the State. Obviously this is a necessary and laudable objective, and it leads to a form of organization in which, appropriately, relationships are highly formalized and ordered, discretion is clearly delineated and the style and form of activities is traditional and conservative. This sounds like the common notion of bureaucracy, and indeed the recognition that such a style of organization is requisite and effective in the appropriate circumstances is important. However, if such an organization tries to develop a new section with very different objectives, or if a new organization is set up in the same general field but with objectives concerned with positive operations or change, then serious problems are likely to occur if the new development is formed with a structure and style based on the original or the notional 'State organization'. An example of this is seen in various countries where a scientific civil service has been set up or has developed on traditional civil service lines but with positive objectives of research and technological advance (which are the antithesis of preservation of the *status quo*). Requisitely such organizations should have a structure and style that enable change to occur, that encourage flexibility and exploration, and this will be very different from the other form that is relevant to other objectives. The spirit rather than the letter will be the prime emphasis, with much more fluid and organic relationships involved, and a managerial style more formally based on co-operation and co-ordination than on authority and direction.

The second feature, perhaps a self-evident one, is that such organizations usually involve public monies and are required to show public accountability. The presence of this requirement or constraint means that the form of the organization's structure concerned with the deployment and use of resources must be relatively formal and codified, with discretion clearly delineated and detailed accountability firmly recognized. Again, this sounds like bureaucracy, and again is appropriate given these conditions. Where the objectives of such an organization involve conservancy and stability, the form of organization to do with public accountability is in natural coherence with the structure for its operations. Where however the organization's objectives are of the more positive kind, such as profitability (as in the case of some State enterprises), developing social services, scientific research, then the form and style of organization structure that is effective in terms of the objectives and the operations that are relevant to them may be in conflict with the form and style to achieve adequate public accountability. This is a well-known conflict, extending in some instances even to university organizations where there has developed (perhaps oversimplified) a classic dichotomy between academic freedom (objectives) and organization form (to give adequate accountability for use of resources, where these are now supplied largely from public sources). An extreme case may occur in a 'scientific civil service' where the organization structure is felt to inhibit scientific work, yet the work itself depends on the availability of very expensive resources, coming from public sources and therefore subject to public accountability. This is not a conflict that cannot be dealt with however; the key is in differential structure. There is no basic reason why public accountability should not be effectively organized and achieved and at the same time a flexibility and freedom of action in operations obtained and encouraged, so long as it is recognized that these different demands require different forms of structure.

The organization's tasks

To design an organization structure, from the basis of the organization's objectives, the organization's main tasks must be identified, and then the structure devised to enable those tasks to be carried out. In this I think lies the crux of broad organization design, because there are two sources of task—the two prime objectives—and both are determined by and at the same time determine relationships with various environmental features. Dealing with the problems that this set of factors presents, recognizing the various options for the form of structure and deciding which to take and when to change—these are the major issues in broad design.

It is essential to recognize that both the output and the capacity objectives always lead to tasks that are concerned with relationships with environmental features as well as having implications for internal relationships. An example is an industrial or commercial business organization. If it is to be successful and survive successfully, then it must be profitable, and it achieves its profit by trading with its market. But it cannot afford to be profitable at all costs; it must invest for the future, it must accept a reduction from maximum short-term profit in order to allow it to protect and develop its resources and facilities. These resources and facilities however basically originate in the organization's environment, which supplies it with materials, human resources, services, finance, equipment and so on. Both the objectives require tasks to be carried out which concern relationship with the environment, tasks to do with relating with the market in one case, with relating with the suppliers of resources and facilities in the other.

A different example might be a local authority social service. If it is to be effective, it must supply the service for which it has been set up, to the public or to the particular recipients within the general public. But it must also relate with the ratepayers, through their representatives, because they supply the financial resource needed to continue the service, and with other environmental factors that affect other necessary resources or their development.

Inadequate terminology can lead to confusion in designing for the interaction between an organization and a particular aspect of its environment. An example of this is sometimes met in the situation of relationship between an organization and its customers, or market, or clients. The term 'marketing' for instance has more than one meaning. The term 'client' may mean different things to the different people concerned with the client. Who are the clients of a hospital? Is it the sick, or also those who at present are well but need the service to be available in case they become sick? Is it on the other hand the doctors, relating directly with their patients and being given a service from the hospital? Does 'marketing' cover only those aspects of the relationship between the commercial firm and its market that are directly to do with the market, or does it cover all the factors in that relationship, including issues such as product development, pricing, quality and selling?

There is no right answer to any of these questions; what matters is that they should be faced, and answered as appropriately and clearly as can be achieved at the time, and the answers modified or changed when necessary.

Operational tasks

The tasks that follow from the organization's output objective may be called the operational tasks. It is usually relatively easy to see conceptually what these tasks must be, but not perhaps so easy to be adequately specific about them.

In general, organizations are profitable, or grow, or become more powerful, or more respected, or attract more members, or deal with a need (and each of these kinds of result applies to different sorts of organizations, and there are many others) mainly by trading with a market, supplying goods or services to a recipient, relating with clients, attracting the public, impressing the Government, and so on. Whatever the form of the environmental feature, the properties of the relationship can be identified conceptually and designed for, as described in Part I.

The thing that is usually more difficult in practice is to define what market the organization should be in, who should be its clients, what 'the public' really means, and what precisely the goods or services should be. Many organizations in all fields have failed to be successful or effective because they failed to answer these questions appropriately.

It is essential to identify accurately which environmental feature is involved and what the content of the relationship is, in terms of the organization's output objective, if the organization design is to be adequately based. In the case of the business organization, this means that the business it is in must be identified adequately, and if it changes this must be recognized. In the case of a service organization, what the service really is required to be must be established. Without this kind of clarity, the balance of effort, the emphasis and the structure itself cannot be designed properly.

Sir Arnold Weinstock, who would be regarded to date as a successful top manager in industry, is reported to have defined the prime task of top management in such an organization as the definition of the market and the product to meet it. He is also reported to be constantly concerned to ensure that the basics of the business are working efficiently and then letting his managers get on with it. I hope he is also concerned with tasks to do with the capacity objective, but he has certainly indicated the operational tasks clearly enough, in his field of organization.

The question of what business an organization is in seems a simple one, but some of the classic failures of organization have been due to misconceptions about this. Sometimes the obvious answer to the question is wrong, or too limited. For example, it seems easy to identify a shop as being in the 'selling business'. If the relationship between the shop and its clientèle is analysed properly however, it becomes clear that the shop is just as much in the business of buying, collecting together and presenting information about what goods are available to its customers as actually selling to them. The idea of the supermarket comes from this recognition, as does an understanding of what the problem of the small village shop often is—plenty of goods to sell, but the customers cannot see the full extent of what is available and the staff cannot find it.

Another example is the engineering firm that describes itself as a manufacturer of engines. The real situation may be that it assembles engines, making some of the component parts itself and buying in others. Because it thinks of itself as an engine manufacturer however, the managerial skill and status may be more related to the actual manufacturing aspect than to what may be more important, the buying of components, their storage and subsequent association with components made in the firm, and presentation to the assembly floor as kits of parts.

One dilemma in all organizations is the extent to which the organization should relate itself to meeting market requirements, client needs, and the extent to which it should try to exploit to the full the resources it possesses. Here again, there is no right answer. Going towards either extreme is generally likely to be dangerous; taking either as the main determinant is likely to be fatal.

Having identified the market, or its equivalent, and the sort of business or field of activity the organization is in, the spelling out of the actual operational tasks that must be carried out, and therefore designed for, follows the conceptual analysis of the features of relationship between the organization and any of the significant entities in its environment. There are however certain points to be observed and pitfalls to be avoided in this. Reference back to Figure 9 will show that the operational tasks fall into three groups:—

There are those to do with the entities in the relationship—identifying what they are and how they are changing, attempting to change them or encourage them to change in a way that is desirable from the organization's point of view.

Others are to do with the content of the transaction—producing the goods or services, establishment of goodwill, development of improved or different goods or services, and so on.

Others again are to do with the process of the transaction—selling, collecting payment, and so on.

In some organizations there is the utmost confusion between these various tasks, largely because terms are used which do not adequately delineate what the tasks inferred really are. There is no alternative to adequate relationship analysis if an organization design is to be effective, because this identifies what tasks must be carried out and how they should relate with each other.

In simple terms, it is usually possible to identify the way in which an organization positively attempts to achieve its output objectives. This way may change through time, but it is normally identifiable at a point in time. In most industrial and commercial firms, for example, the intention is that the objective of profit shall be secured by trading with the market, in the widest sense. This is not to say that other work, such as is involved in relating with sources of capital, or with employees, does not materially or even sometimes overwhelmingly affect profit, but it is a recognition that the organization is geared to trading with the market.

This relationship between the organization and the market can be analysed and the operational tasks that follow can be recognized. In a sense there is nothing fundamental about these; they are what are involved at a given point in time, and the boundaries between them are the results of decisions as to how to delineate them. It is extremely helpful however to identify them in a given situation, for without identification and consequent decisions as to how to structure and manage them, the organization's control of the achieving of its objectives is bound to be inadequate.

Tasks concerned with the capacity objective

The capacity objective leads to tasks concerned with resources and facilities, with obtaining them, maintaining them, training them, safeguarding them, developing them, changing them. Terminology again is a problem here. These tasks are sometimes called 'specialist' tasks, though they may not necessarily be the only ones that need specialists to carry them out, and this can lead to considerable confusion. Sometimes they are lumped together, under the heading of 'administration', or 'services', and sometimes they are called 'staff' tasks, related with the 'line' tasks that as usually identified are a narrow version of what are here being called the operational tasks. None of these terms is fully adequate, and each invites misconception which can be very damaging because it often concerns questions of authority. Perhaps the rational term for these tasks is 'other' or 'non-operational', because they are contrasted with the operational tasks, but the expression I will use here for them is 'resource-based'.

The focus of the resource-based tasks is resources and facilities. These fall into two main categories, as identified in Part I, and each of the categories—working resources and enabling resources—has a number of elements in it. The resource-based tasks in an organization therefore are to do with the money, the information, the human resource, the physical resources and their technical features, the time resource, as resources rather than in terms of their direct use in output tasks. How these resource-based tasks should be designated into roles, and what role-relationships should be designed, follows an analysis of the resources and facilities in the organization and how they are used in the organization's work. It is necessary however to recognize that there are likely to be two kinds of resource-based task. There are tasks concerned with the resources and facilities in use in the organization; the maintenance of the organization's plant, the personnel and training tasks related to the people who work in the organization, the financial administration within the organization, are examples. There are also tasks concerned with the obtaining of resources from the environment of the organization; interaction with Trade Unions, the obtaining of finance, the purchasing of plant, are examples. Often these kinds of tasks exist together in the same unit or function, and sometimes this juxtaposition causes confusion and distortion of authority. The tasks are obviously connected with each other, but in an effective organization, design confusion will be prevented by a clear differentiation between them whether they are then allocated to the same roles or whether (as is often the case in larger organizations) they are separated into different roles. An example is often seen in the financial field. Administration of the financial resource within the organization is connected with but different from the obtaining of finance. The former, because it is in effect a service, is often a lower-level task than the latter which may be a determinant of the organization's survival. The status of the latter task may distort the authority in the former if they are carried out in the same roles and the distinction between them is not clear.

II.3 Forms of organization design

Conventional forms of organization design

Now let us look at conventional structures. Very broadly, there are three forms. Various terms are used by different people and in different fields of organization, but basically the three forms boil down to the following:—

The functional form. In this the organization structure is determined by the kind of training, the disciplines or the personal functions of those who work within it.

The executive/administrative form. In this type of structure there is a separation between the organization of the work that manifests itself in output to the customer or client and the organization of all the other internal functions that together form the 'administration' work.

The line/staff form. Here the structure of the organization for the output work (the 'line' structure) is linked with a number of 'staff' structures, each dealing with particular aspects of that work, or of the particular resources involved in it. A developed version is the operational specialist form, in which 'operational' functions are identified from analysis of the relationship between the organization and, in the case of an industrial firm for example, its market (usually production selling and development) and these are linked with 'specialist' functions concerned with the particular aspects of work (often personnel, technical, programming, finance, information). This of course is approaching the basic form that emerges as a result of conceptual analysis.

The functional form

Many organizations are structured like this, often because this is the way in which they have grown. New roles are developed, new departments set up, because particular additional skills, knowledge, professional disciplines are needed in the organization, and these become the determinants of structure. An example is often seen in the situation where people from different professions are employed. An engineering consultancy firm may develop as a result of the skill of say a civil engineer. He builds up a civil engineering practice, but then discovers perhaps that some of the work his firm is offered is in the field of mechanical engineering. A senior mechanical engineer is then recruited, and builds up a mechanical

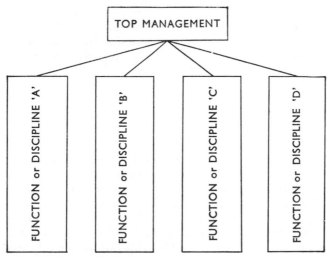

Figure 11—Simple functional structure

engineering department alongside the existing civil engineering department. The same thing may happen with other fields of engineering professionalism, and no doubt also the need appears, for other reasons, for an accounting department, perhaps a computer department, and so on. The result over the years is the evolution of a functional form of organization (Figure 11). This will be effective as a structure so long as the work of the organization can be delegated adequately into the different departments, with co-ordination between their efforts or services given by departments to other departments as required. As soon as inter-functional projects appear however, or the stresses of co-ordination and services become too high, this form of organization becomes inadequate. Basically, this form is related to the operations of the

G

different functions and not primarily to the demands of the work that the organization is set up to do, and this is its inherent weakness. Its strength is that there is a consistency of function in each department. People with certain skills, certain disciplines, tend to be managed by people with similar skills or disciplines, with an understanding of the susceptibilities and attitudes of those they are managing. Thus attention to career planning, training, professional standards, tends to be good. Resources tend to be well managed, as resources, and attention to such things as maintenance and development tend to be good. This form of organization in practice tends to be increasingly unsatisfactory as time goes on from the point of view of the real work being required of the organization. This is particularly so if in the past it has been successful in its work, because this success is likely to have led to demands for more complex work, bigger projects, inter-disciplinary effort.

The executive/administrative form

This form of structure is related to the work demands on the organization, but its weakness is often that the separation between the 'executive' side and the 'administrative' side becomes unrealistic and the source of much unnecessary conflict. This is especially likely where the task of the administrative side of the total operation is more than to service the executive side, but to control it to some extent. In some organizations what happens is almost that the administrative side holds the purse-strings whilst the executive side carries the accountability for results, and this separation or part-separation between those accountable for results and those controlling a vital resource is inevitably dangerous unless exceedingly good co-operation can be achieved between them.

Furthermore, what sometimes happens is that departments are built up, not to achieve output work but to relate with specific resources—personnel and training departments, professional or technological departments for example—and these come into conflict with administration, because their activities overlap, unless very careful sorting out of roles is achieved and well-defined policies established to govern the interactions.

A basic fault in some organizations of this type is that their executive side is no longer related to the present work demands on the organization but only to those in the past, which have now changed. In this situation, no improvement in the existing form of structure is likely to be of any consequence; what is needed is complete re-structuring.

The line/staff form

In essence the line/staff form is a development of the executive/ administrative form, in that the line structure is based, or should be based, on the work demand on the organization. There are two basic problems in a line/staff design. One is the problem of authority in staff roles, and this question of the authority of specialists in their relationship with managers has already been discussed. The other is the problem of identifying what the work demands on the organization are in order to see what the line structure should be based on and what its orientation should be. Line structures tend to be 'production oriented' or 'sales oriented' or 'research oriented', but as soon as it is recognized that the work demand on an organization comes from its relationship with its environment, then the recognition that line structure should be one of multiple function emerges. This is the basis of the more developed operational/

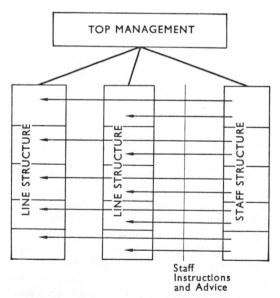

Figure 12—Simple line/staff form

specialist form of design; there are three functions involved in the relationship with the market, or the client. This more advanced version however is now becoming inadequate in some organizations which are having to relate effectively and positively at times with other significant features of their environment, which thus imply other operational functions than the normal ones. The basic line/ staff form is shown in Figure 12.

Inadequacies of conventional forms

In many organizations, the conventional forms of structure, with modifications in detail, still remain effective, but inadequacies that can no longer be absorbed within responsible behaviour or by informal means are often beginning to appear. In some cases, these inadequacies are so great that major re-organization rather than improvement in conventional forms is needed. All the conventional forms, except in very simple situations, tend to encourage bias of status between different functions or different departments (for example 'line' may have higher status than 'staff', more say in policy-making, not because of competence or real importance but because it is 'line'). They tend to infer that because some functions are more directly linked than others with the objectives of the organization, those others can be sacrificed or cut down more readily and safely when things get tight. They all tend to be unsatisfactory, either from the point of view of the real work demand on the organization or from the point of view of the need for effective management and development of resources.

The matrix form of organization

A new form of organization structure, or, rather, a further logical development that is now beginning to appear is the matrix design. This has evolved and is beginning to be applied in various fields of organization largely as a result of experience of the shortcomings of conventional structures that have already been discussed.

The matrix design in essence is one in which there is a set of project or task structures based on the work demands on the organization, changing as those work demands change, superimposed on a structure or set of structures concerned with the facilities or resources involved in the organization (this is shown in Figure 13). It is perhaps easiest to envisage this form of organization in circumstances where the output of the organization is in the form of specific projects, and it is in such situations that the first practical examples of matrix structure are appearing, in the aerospace industry, in large civil engineering project organizations, in research companies and the like. Facilities or resources are allocated into

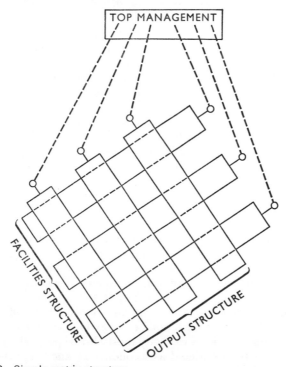

Figure 13—Simple matrix structure

projects as required, and are there directly managed by the project organization; when no longer required in the project their control reverts to the 'facilities' structure (for training, maintenance, reallocation for example), and this goes on within an envelope of overall distribution of control of the particular facility or resource as determined by top management. The objective of the matrix design in this kind of situation is to ensure that a proper and controlled balance is struck between the pressures of the projects and the pressures to do with development of resources. The approach starts from the recognition that the organization has two competing basic objectives, one to do with output and one to do with the capacity that enables the output to continue. In the simplest matrix form, inter-connected sets of structures of equal status are established; one set relates to outputs, the other set to facilities. The authority relationship between these sets of structures follows from top management decisions about the distribution of effort between the output objectives and the capacity objectives. The actual source of management of a particular facility or resource changes from time to time, and is determined at any particular point in time by whether the facility or resource at that point is operating in the output work structure or in the facilities structure.

The crucial aspect of matrix structure is the role of top management. It is essential that the decisions about balance of effort between the two structures are made clearly and communicated, and this is not an easy matter because it exposes perhaps the most important aspects of pure judgment in an organization, the allocation of effort between output and capacity objectives.

Detailed design

Once the form of the broad structure of the organization is established, in the sense of the structural response to the organization's objectives, the internal organizational details may be designed, using the design elements of role, managerial role and so on to achieve this. It is obvious I think that the operational tasks be effectively managed, since the organization's direct effectiveness depends on this. What may not be so obvious is that the tasks to do with the organization's capacity must also be properly managed. They must not be considered as secondary or ancillary; the managerial problems they present may be as complex as those in the operational functions, and the resources involved in carrying out these tasks may well be greater or more expensive on occasion than those in the operational tasks. As the technology in organizations becomes more advanced, a frequent result is a reduction in numbers and levels of people involved in the operational side of things and an increase in the numbers and levels of people concerned with maintenance, training, information processing, administration and other non-operational work.

A consequent point that causes some difficulty unless there is conceptual clarity is this. Within both the operational tasks and resource-based tasks (at the level of the organization as a whole) there are consequential output and capacity objectives, so that right through the organization, there are tasks to do with 'output' and tasks to do with 'capacity', coming together level by level to form the totality of work, as was indicated in Figure 10. This is so, whether these different tasks are allocated into separate roles or whether they exist side by side in the same role.

Delegation

The question of delegation crops up in many discussions about organization design. However well an organization is structured in situational terms, in terms of roles and relationships between roles, the process of delegation is also needed if the organization is to be effective. Delegation goes on in all real organizations, though sometimes it is not recognized as such, or happens by default rather than by intention. It is the process of assigning work to someone else to perform, and thus it involves requiring or allowing decisions to be made by others.

Delegation must occur in fact to the extent that more than one person is involved in an organization's work. Even in the case where the people in the organization together decide what is to be done, the actual implementation of their decision will inevitably require them to allocate specific work to individuals, in other words in delegation. Even at the other extreme, where the organization is run by one person at the top, who issues orders to everyone else, delegation really occurs, though the person at the top may deny this. He may think he is telling the others, his subordinates, precisely what to do, but in reality there are limits beyond which this is not possible; some freedom of action is inevitably left to those subordinates, if not indeed demanded by them. It is in this essential possession of individual freedom that the human resource is different from the machine.

Basically then there are two reasons for delegation, one to do with pressure, volume and complexity or variety of work, the other with the particular properties of the human resource. Conscious and effective delegation is thus a feature of all effective organizations. Once this is recognized, then the question becomes not whether to delegate but how far to delegate and what must be involved.

The delegation of work to another person is not a shedding of accountability for that work by the person delegating, nor a sharing of that accountability, but its temporary allocation to another, within the overall accountability of the person delegating. Delegation therefore implies authority—the person delegating must have the authority to do so if the delegation is to be effective.

Delegation of accountability for work is likely to be vague and inadequate unless it is in the form of delegation of tasks. Tasks are always bounded by certain limits, set by policies, procedures and instructions, and by the boundaries of the tasks themselves, in terms of their objectives, of the limits of available resources and the limits of the activities to be carried out; effective delegation thus always involves a communication of the relevant boundaries. Resources must be deployed, resources of material and equipment, human resources, time, perhaps money and information. Delegation which does not include all the necessary resources is ineffective; for example if a delegated task needs money to be spent, information to be used, time, people and equipment to carry it out, then authority must be delegated to spend money, have access to the necessary information, use the time and equipment and manage the people involved. This is another way of saying that delegation of work is of little real meaning without the necessary deployment of resources, because the work that actually can be done is determined by the effective resources available; delegation of accountability must be allied to delegation of authority to use the resources required. Delegation of authority does not mean that the person delegating it is losing it, but rather that within the limits of his authority of access to resources there is a delegation of that access to someone else.

In order to use resources and to do work, decisions must be made, and so delegation is basically the delegation of authority to make those decisions, and of accountability for their outcome. An important boundary of delegation is that in time; subordinates carry out activities subject to their manager's view of their performance—this is the meaning of accountability. If the manager's review of work is made too soon, then the subordinate feels that the nominal delegation has in fact been rescinded. If review is at too great a time-interval for the capacity of the subordinate to stand, then the subordinate feels inadequately supported by the manager. Thus if a manager delegates work and deploys appropriate resources, but reviews that work inappropriately, then this is not effective delegation.

There is a limit to what can be delegated, set by the boundaries of work in the role of the person delegating. Another limit to what can be effectively delegated is set by the boundaries of authority, of access to resources. A further limit is in the capacity of the individual to whom the work is delegated, and the kind of role he is in. There is a limit to the number of subordinates that a manager can adequately manage, determined partly by the work-content of their roles and partly by the organizational and personal relationships in the situation. The availability of specialists may have a big effect on delegation since they may assist a manager adequately to manage a greater range of resources, or on the other hand they may interfere with this. Clarity of authority relationships between specialists and managers is thus vital.

Among the influences affecting delegation adversely are lack of clarity of organization structure, and persisting factors or traditions which become inappropriate for or incompatible with the work to be done. For effective delegation there must be effective communication and there must be a sense of responsibility—no delegation is effective, however well achieved organizationally, unless the person to whom the work is delegated carries the accountability with a sense of responsibility or commitment.

When a manager has delegated a task to a subordinate, he meets a problem of control. If he doesn't leave the subordinate to get on with the task, he is beginning to take over from the subordinate; he is interfering. If he does leave the subordinate to get on with it, he may be taking a big risk in that the subordinate may be carrying out the task wrongly or inadequately. There is no one answer, or right answer, to the question of how to strike a balance between the need to delegate and the need to reduce risk to an acceptable level, but once this is recognized as a problem of control and the factors identified then the manager can see how to achieve an adequate balance.

The subordinate's task is to meet the objective required by using his resources as effectively as he can to carry out the relevant activities. By watching the way the results of his activities move towards the objective, he obtains the feedback that allows him to steer his progress in the task, by redeploying resources, adjusting activities where necessary. This is a cybernetic process. The manager in a similar cybernetic way sets the boundaries of his subordinate's freedom of action and observes the way the subordinate moves towards his objectives. This feedback of review allows the manager to decide whether or not to adjust the relationship between delegation and risk. The major review of course is of task completion, and it must be a review of the effect on resources (that is, 'cost') of completing the task, as well as review of the quality of the result achieved. This view of managerial control as a cybernetic process shows why the time span of a subordinate's work seems so significant —it is the time scale of autonomous control. The relationship between manager and subordinate is the interaction of two perceptions, in a cybernetic process. The subordinate 'does the work'— he controls, steers his use of resources to move towards his objective. The manager is concerned with the same work, but in the abstract so long as he delegates it (more accurately, the control of it) to his subordinate. He plans it and regulates it, closing in on the subordinate or opening out depending on the feedback he gets and his experience of this subordinate.

In some situations, another cybernetic factor is present, in the form of a 'critical path' method of planning work. Serious conflicts have developed on occasion where it has not been recognized that there are then two control mechanisms operating—the critical path programme and the managerial control—with similar features. By recognizing both, and understanding their interaction, these conflicts between manager, subordinate and plan can be minimized.

Centralization and decentralization

A subject that seems particularly prone to opinion, and indeed swings of fashion, is that of centralization and decentralization. Forty years ago, for example, a Papal Bull asserted:—

It is indeed true, as history clearly proves, that owing to changed circumstances much that was formerly done by small groups can nowadays only be done by large associations. None the less, just as it is wrong to withdraw from the individual and commit to a group what private enterprise and industry can accomplish, so too it is an injustice, a grave evil and a disturbance of right order, for a larger and higher association to abrogate to itself functions which can be performed efficiently by smaller and lower societies. This is a fundamental principle of social philosophy, unshaken and unchangeable. Of its very nature the true aim of all social activity should be to help members of the social body, but never to destroy or absorb them.

It went on to say:—

The State, therefore, would leave to smaller groups the settlement of business of minor importance, which otherwise would greatly distract it; it will thus carry out with greater freedom, power and success the tasks belonging to it alone, because it alone can effectively accomplish these; directing, watching, stimulating, restraining, as circumstances suggest and necessity demands. Let those in power, therefore, be convinced that the more faithfully this principle of subsidiary function be followed, and a graded hierarchical order exist between various associations, the greater will be both social authority and social efficiency, and the happier and more prosperous the condition of the commonwealth.

The 'principle of subsidiarity' indicated in those words seems to give an accurate view of the real issue, which is not whether organizations should be centralized or decentralized but to what degree or extent authority should be decentralized. There is no such thing as an organization that is not decentralized to some degree; the concept of management and the unique feature of the human resource— that it has free will—establish this. But there is no such thing either as an organization without central direction and coherence. The question is, how much. A good maxim concerning the interaction between the centre and the periphery is 'as much freedom as possible, as much intervention as necessary'.

A helpful way to think about an organization in this respect is as a flywheel, with centrifugal forces due to the motion of the periphery trying to pull it apart, and centripetal forces designed into the construction holding it together and preventing it from flying to pieces.

Expansion of work or greater delegation of autonomy towards the periphery must be balanced by adequate control from the centre if decentralization is not to lead to incoherence by default.

What I think matters above all in this whole question of decentralization is that the centre, or top management, shall make those decisions that only it can make, and exercise that control that only it can exercise, delegating the rest as far as possible, and this means as far as competence and confidence in the situation allows.

If decentralization is to mean anything, it must be decentralization of authority, because if managers are to carry accountability effectively they must know that they are in control of the resources and facilities they need to use. In order to keep this control adequately 'anchored' in the organization however, their control of resources should be in the light of the programme or plan or task for which they are accountable, and this should be agreed with them. Their performance can then be maintained accordingly. 'Control of necessary resources' does not mean that all services must come under the managerial control of the manager accountable for the programme, but he must have the final control on how and when they are used, within policies setting out the general delineation of such usage.

Decentralization of decision-making means decentralization of risk-taking. One aspect of this may be seen for example when the risk is to do, say, with the way an external project is handled, particularly sharply in financial terms. The risk in the project would appear only capable of assessment in the field, where the decision-maker is in direct contact with the project environment. But this does not deal with the risk to the organization as a whole, which can only be assessed at the top of the organization. Thus there is a 'risk-dilemma' which cannot be solved by centralization or by decentralization, but by both, with an adequate understanding of the interdependency of the two. This means that communications must be good, and confidence between the central and decentralized decision-makers must be present.

If decentralization means geographical distance, or relative autonomy, as well as organizational autonomy, an accentuated problem may occur. With relative autonomy of units, the central bodies are often only called in for advice or assistance when a situation has become critical, rather than as part of an on-going relationship. (The relationship is intermittent, and problem-centred, in other words.) With geographical proximity, the central bodies may achieve a sense of what is going on, without cutting across the autonomy of the units, but when geographical distance also intervenes then this 'informal safeguard' does not exist.

Decentralization is often the result of or response to an increase in size of the organization, for inevitably such increase means that central control must gradually yield to localized autonomy, because of the increase in the number of roles and relationships involved and the development of longer chains of communication and so on. Large organizations are more vulnerable to changes outside their control, if they are not decentralized, because they are less sensitive to what is happening and less quick to react.

This process however should be designed; decentralization should not happen by default. By design, decentralization must not occur before the managers who will operate with more local autonomy have been identified as adequate, and this means that decisions about what is to be decentralized must be taken and communication to and training of those key managers achieved.

This centrifugal movement must be watched carefully, because once established it tends to accelerate. The more competent and effective and capable of development the key managers are, the more likely is this acceleration to occur, and it may become difficult to hold the organization together if the release of creative talent at the periphery of the organization becomes too great.

A particular aspect of the issues and problems of decentralization may be seen in the relationship between the centre of a large organization and major units in it. An example is the relationship in a large business firm between the main company and its subsidiaries.

Main difficulties are likely to be to do with:—

differing views of the extent of autonomy of the subsidiary;
interaction between main company staff and the subsidiary's management;
different styles of management and different cultures as between main company and subsidiary.

Each of these areas may be particularly affected if the subsidiary is geographically separated or even in a different country from the main company.

In terms of the first area of difficulty, the expectation of the subsidiary is often very different from that of the main company, which may require the subsidiary to achieve profitability whilst detailed control of certain aspects of the subsidiary's operations may be retained in the main company. This problem is often accentuated by the second; main company staff may have an influence on their opposite numbers in the subsidiary which can interfere with the direct managerial situation between main and subsidiary company. This is often seen, when it happens, in the financial area, but areas such as research and development and personnel can also show this feature.

The relationship between a main company and a subsidiary can be anywhere between the subsidiary having complete freedom of action, controlled only by investment and a profit objective, to the subsidiary being completely controlled by the main company in all aspects of its operations so that it has practically no freedom of action at all. What seems to matter is not so much where the freedom lies on this continuum, but that it is understood in the same way by both sides, that it is balanced across all the aspects of the subsidiary's operations and above all that accountability is matched by real authority of usage of resources.

It is essential that the question of style and culture is understood by both sides, and it is essential to distinguish between the style of relationship and their content, for the distinction may be different as between different cultures.

A problem sometimes met is that of bias in decentralization, and there are two versions of it. In one version, certain decisions are decentralized but others, which may be felt in the subsidiary or at the periphery to be equally validly decentralized are not. In a sense, autonomy is indivisible, and differential decentralization or delegation should not be designed unless there are very strong reasons for it. In the other version, subsidiaries or units that seem to be of equivalent status have different levels of autonomy; the decentralization of authority is different. This differentiation may be entirely justified and appropriate if it is based on different competences or different performances in the subsidiaries.

Organization and professional work

A basic design point is that of the reconciliation between the interests and requirements of the organization and those of the people in it. This can become particularly sharp when the individuals concerned are vital resources and have an attitude to their work which is not identical with that of the organization. In the situation, for example, where professional work is being done, there may be an organizational need for clear control of resources, especially if the resources are expensive, or involve public monies. On the other hand, the activities engaged in may involve the individual in considerable autonomy, whether the initiative for this comes from the organization's definition of work or from the individual's demand for autonomy. Thus the reconciliation needed may be in a situation of potentially fairly severe conflict. Effective organization structure will recognize this, and one of the logical manifestations of this recognition is that organizational definition and managerial control will tend to concentrate on the allocation of resources and review of their use, and on definition of objectives, rather than on definition of activities and even on performance, leaving these latter to the individual and ensuring their adequacy by achieving adequate competence, confidence and motivation.

A further point may then be made. There is a distinction between professional work done in an organization set up to do that work, and apparently exactly the same work done in an organization which is part of a larger organization. This latter can be the case, for example, where a project team is set up within an organization, or where an organization has a professional department within its general organization. The distinction begins with objectives; in the case of the professional organization, the determinants and constraints on its objectives are environmental, whereas when the work is part of a larger organization there are also internal organizational factors that affect objectives, since they are (or should be) a consequence of the objectives of the larger organization. Thus in the second case, the organization structure, the policies and procedures, and the managerial style in the professional area are affected by or even sometimes determined by those of the larger organization, and to this extent cannot be designed entirely to suit the professional work. There tends thus to be more tension between the particular work and personal requirements and the organizational features in a professional department or a project department that is part of a larger organization, than when the organization is specifically for such work. To achieve as good a situation as possible therefore in the professional department, recognition of the differences, at least in degree, between the professional situation and the more general organizational one is essential so that an affective compromise between organizational consistency and the particular features of professional work can be achieved.

This is a general issue where what may broadly be called professional work is involved. People with professional skills are often jealous of their autonomy, because the way they can use it is the major resource in the situation, as they see it. All work in an organization however should be related to the organization's objectives, and this applies to professional work as to any other. In some situations however the organization's objectives are one or more stages removed from those of the professional work itself, whilst in others the organization's objectives *are* those of the professional work. This may seem quite a small distinction, but since the design of the organization and the style and techniques of management follow from the objectives of the organization, as well as from the kind of work and people involved, different results ensue. In the first kind of situation, where the organization's objectives are somewhat removed from the direct objectives in the professional work itself, there will always be an 'organizational dichotomy' of style, standards and priorities between the organizational and the professional aspects. In the second, there may be problems of course within the professional work situation, to do perhaps with control, or with the interaction between the technological and the economic aspects, but there is no basic problem of the first kind.

Product or market managers

A design issue occurs in some organizations where there is a multiplicity of products or services, or a multiplicity of markets for the same product or service. In the case of the manufacturing firm where there are various products manufactured flowing into a common market through the same channels, it is usual to establish 'product manager' roles, in which the aim is to develop accountability for planning and achieving the effectiveness of each product or product segment. Where different markets need to be developed for a single product, then 'market manager' roles usually emerge. In these, the accountability is for the development of the particular market segment. Whichever way the firm is structured however, it should recognize that it is implicitly or explicitly deciding how to deal with the classic problem mentioned earlier—should we primarily follow what the market wants, and try to exploit that need, or should we primarily try to exploit the resources we possess, to the full, encouraging the market to need what this exploitation produces? It is essential that this underlying question be reviewed from time to time and not lost by default because of the organization structure of 'product' or 'market'.

More firms now however are meeting the fact that the dilemma cannot and must not be 'solved' one way or the other, but must be kept as a constant interaction. This leads to the view that both product and market manager roles may be required together. In this situation of duality, the former is product focused and has the objective of achieving a balanced response to the needs and opportunities of certain markets in relation to others, in the light of the load on production. The latter is externally focused, and has the objective of improving understanding of market needs and how they are changing, and how the firm can become more responsive to those needs. The problem then is that these roles are inherently in conflict or competition, and it is essential that the top management defines them adequately and sets policies about their interactions.

Planning

The form of planning, as a process, and the results of that process—the organization's plans—have a major impact on organization design, and the design of the organization structure conversely affects planning very much. Sometimes this interaction is not recognized, and the credibility of planning or the status of the organization structure become damaged as a result.

One effect of good planning in an organization is that the plan can and should become the basis of the control of operations. The justification for activities comes from the plan, rather than from direct managerial instructions. Control can become 'self-control', on the basis of the agreed plan, and maintained in terms of that plan. This infers a philosophy of maximum delegation of autonomy, and of an objective basis of management (even though that objective basis, the plan, is itself the result of much subjectivity and judgment). If this is to be achieved, then adequate dialogue between the manager accountable for carrying out the plan and his manager is essential. The initiative for this dialogue must be shared however, or preferably more on the side of the subordinate manager, otherwise 'control' rather than 'self-control' creeps back into the situation. The plan may need to have contingency allowances built into it, but these should not be too extensive or they will destroy the status of the plan. If major contingencies might be a possibility, it is better to develop a second plan—a contingency plan *per se*.

Obviously, all this has design implications, in terms of both structure and style in the organization.

H

II.4 Organization style

An explicit approach to organization design has implications for what I want to call 'organization style'. The general way in which people behave and relate with one another, the style of management and leadership, the attitude to problems and inadequacies—these are all elements of the general organization style that have a direct relationship with the form of organization structure and with the way in which that form is communicated to the people who operate in and with it.

The life, the action in an organization comes from the people in it, acting individually and in groups. The organization's structure should give a framework, a degree of consistency, to this action. At the same time, this structure is itself affected by those people who work in the organization. As soon as behaviour or relationships become consistent or routine, they become structured, implicitly or explicitly, and this aspect of structure relates, positively or conflictingly, with the organization structure. Organization structure is then both a determinant of behaviour and a product of behaviour, and a recognition of the interaction is essential if an organization is to be effectively designed. Knowledge of how people work, how they respond to work, how they relate with each other in work, is the field of behavioural science, but this knowledge must be linked with an understanding of work itself, its processes and their organization, if it is to be used effectively.

The behaviour of people is affected broadly by two factors. One is inherent in the person or group, and involves the individual personality, or the group culture. The other factor is the perception that the individual or group possesses of the circumstances within which he or it exists and works.

In the context of an organization, therefore, behaviour is affected by the perceived organizational factors as well as by the purely human ones.

It is no good having someone in an inadequately designed role and expecting to put things right by good human relationships. As a major factor in its effect on behaviour, the person's role must be adequately perceived and what is perceived must be acceptable or at least tolerable to that person. A manager may understand the role he wants his subordinate to fill, but unless he can communicate it in meaningful terms then the perception of the subordinate is not likely to be adequately based.

The role itself must be satisfactory, in terms of work (objectives and resources as well as activities being clear). Thus authority and accountability must be properly delegated. The level of work must be appropriate for the capacity of the person in the role. The reward for the role must be satisfactory to that person, and this means it must be understood, and differentially appropriate.

The other determinant of behaviour is the inherent one. But such factors as personality and its aspects are linked with the situation which they operate—'good' qualities in one situation may be irrelevant or negative in another. Some facets of personality (such as the desire for status, for power) may take advantage of an organizational situation and bias it further away from what is appropriate. If the person concerned is also a member of a group or groups, then group norms as well as purely personal factors affect this determinant.

The case for formalizing organization structure has already been discussed. A structure that has no degree of formalization about it requires properties in the people involved that are not likely to be present in real human beings. On the other hand, a completely formalized structure leaves no escape routes from intolerable aspects of the organization or work.

One question which often arises when there is an explicit or formal structure, especially in terms of policies, directives, procedures (that is, process structure), is whether people should always operate 'to the letter', or whether they should use common sense, sense of responsibility or expediency in 'bending the rules', 'cutting corners', and dealing with particular problems in the light of their own merits. The two different approaches are not so mutually incompatible as the terms used to infer, yet nevertheless the underlying question represents an element of organizational philosophy which needs exploration.

It is axiomatic that a structure or rule, law or policy that cannot

be enforced or respected—that does not achieve an order or dis-
cipline, externally or self-induced—is bad and should be changed.
But the testing out of structure in order to ascertain whether it is
effective can only be done by trial and error. If people work to the
letter they may be charged with having a mechanistic approach,
or with a lack of humanity. Yet it is only by working in this way
that inadequacies are exposed in the constitutions, policies or rules,
and a humane approach to dealing with such inadequacies then
developed. If on the other hand, common sense, sense of responsibility or expediency is used to bend the rules then a better immediate
result may be achieved. But the price paid for this is that inadequacies
in the formal framework are not exposed, and thus the rules and
policies gradually come into disrepute, with damage thus ensuing
to the organization and subsequently to people in it.

The dilemma is really between the two ways of achieving change
in an organization, the short-term way and the long-term way. The
long-term way is to work to the organization structure, exposing
its properties and effects and then changing it explicitly. This
is change by *evolution*. The other way is to ignore the organization structure where it is felt to be inadequate, and use *ad hoc*
common sense or sense of responsibility to deal with problems.
The outcome is debilitation of the status of the structure, and
eventually the achievement of change by destruction (i.e. change
by *revolution*).

A practical way to compromise between these extremes is to
make sure that when a rule or other structural feature is broken
to achieve a good immediate result, this is reported straightaway
and amendment proposed. It is worth remembering that however
great is the inadequacy in the structure or policy from the point
of view of the person challenging it in a specific instance, there
is likely to have been some reasoning or rationality behind its
establishment. Thus a refusal to apply it, because it is inadequate, offends common sense, or is difficult to understand perhaps,
implies a confrontation with its initiators and supporters and a
challenge to some of the reasoning which may have been perfectly
competent. Yet the desire to refuse to co-operate may be very
strong, and based on a sense of responsibility which is equally
competent. Once this is recognized, a more effective, humane and
generally competent situation can be developed, salving the con-
science and sense of responsibility of the person who is required to
carry out the policy for example, safeguarding the interests of the
situation within which or to which the policy is applied and at

the same time upholding the status of the policy whilst exposing the need for further clarification or evolution.

One other issue of this nature that sometimes arises is when a rule is broken or an instruction ignored 'for the good of the organization'. This can happen when accountability for a task or duty is considered to be valid only so long as other factors do not get in the way. Sometimes a task is deviated from in order to 'do the organization good' by saving expense. There should always be discretion allowed within a task or duty, as to how to accomplish it, but not to alter the task. There is responsibility to raise the view that a task or duty is in some way inappropriate, but it is one thing to do this at an early stage and quite another to fail to carry out the task delegated and then explain when challenged that it was felt to be in the interests of the organization to do so.

The explicit aspects of the structure in an organization then are only a part of the total structural set. The organization structure in a situational sense, linked with the process structure in terms of policies and procedures, specific mechanisms of consultation and participation, and so on, forms this explicit part of the total. The organizational style—the 'way things are done around here'—and the pattern of behaviour of a particular manager for example—are also factors that may be regarded as structural or as having structural implications. They are structural, even if only implicit and undefined or inconsistent, because they also limit or define the freedom of action of people in the organization.

An understanding of these other kinds of structural or quasi-structural issues is necessary if organizations are to be designed effectively, and this is particularly the case where changes are being made; a change in the explicit structure may run into trouble not because it has been designed inadequately in the explicit sense but because it falls foul of cultural or style constraints in the organization.

An example of the interaction between structure and style is readily seen in the situation of delegation. A manager may delegate to his subordinate a task he wishes carried out; he does this by communicating the task to the subordinate clearly and in effective terms of the result to be aimed at, resources available and boundaries of permitted activities. But if he stands over the subordinate whilst he is performing the task, or checks up too quickly on the way things are going, or offers too much gratuitous advice, then something begins to happen—the subordinate begins to resent the manager's behaviour, which he regards as interference even though the manager may be offering it as 'help'. In this case, the manager's style is interfering with the structure of the situation of the task.

An aspect of this interaction between the elements of structure that are organizational in their basis (in other words, based on the requirements of work) and those that result from the people and their behaviour in the situation can sometimes be seen when an organization tries to 'get itself sorted out'. What often happens is that an improved organization structure is developed, based more effectively on the properties of the work that is required to be done in the organization. As a result, the attention of the people in the organization is drawn more explicitly to their work and its properties, and any inadequacies in that work or in the understanding of it (from the individual's point of view as well as from the organization's) will become more exposed. If the individual's main interest and loyalty is to his work, rather than to his organization, or to his manager, then this exposure of inadequacies can become very troublesome, to an extent that inadequacies and problems which previously were accepted as part of the general scene become resented or intolerable in the new situation. Another version of this effect of improvement of this kind is that the individual whose interest is in his work will have this reinforced, his work becoming the major focus of his loyalty and sense of responsibility. This result of developing a more work-centred or task-oriented organization can be a disconcerting one for some managers who have been used to personal loyalty as the main focus.

One issue of style that often causes difficulty is that of 'putting up proposals for approval'. The question to be answered if the issue is to be dealt with adequately in the organizational sense is 'what is the organizational objective of this proposal? Is it to get higher-level positive agreement (in effect, higher-level accountability for it) or is it to achieve higher-level confirmation that the proposal is within the limits that the higher-level body is willing to accept?' If accountability for the proposal's implementation rather than just its quality is to be carried by those putting it up, then the reaction to the proposal should be of the second kind. If the reaction must be of the first kind, then the accountability implications must be clearly understood by those involved.

This kind of issue can lead to particularly acute problems of conflict in two situations. One is where those putting up the proposal are experts in the field of the proposal, and those considering the proposal are not; the other is where the proposer is an individual and the higher-level body is not. In the first case, the experts may resent it strongly if the higher-level body tries to understand or criticize its technical details in order to agree positively with the proposal, because the level of technical knowledge is not the same. 'Why use experts if they then think they can do it better themselves?' is a comment I have sometimes heard. On the other hand, if the experts understand that the higher-level body is not challenging their expertise but trying to relate the proposal to the widest issues that they are properly concerned with, then this conflict does not arise.

In the second case, as for example when an organization's chief executive puts up a proposal to his Board of Directors, the problem is that the Board cannot carry accountability for the implementation of the proposal, because this is not in its role nor would it be effective if it were, because of the intermittent nature of occupancy of the role of the Board and the composite nature of the role-occupant. The appropriate relationship therefore in terms of recommendations, proposals and the like put up by the lower-level body is to do with the boundaries in the situation, rather than the facts of the proposal. The role of the higher-level body, perhaps a Board, is to ensure that the proposals come within the boundaries of objectives and resources that concern them, in terms of the security and advancement of the organization. This defines the accountability at that level. The role of the lower-level body, perhaps a chief executive, is to make the proposals, and when sanctioned, manage their implementation. This defines the accountability at that level, for the quality of the proposals and for the effectiveness of their implementation. This kind of observation basically follows from recognition that every decision made in an organizational context really represents two decisions—one is the decision in question; the other is the decision which answers the preceding question 'is this decision I wish to make within the boundaries of acceptability to the organization?'. In other words, every piece of work, or every decision, has two aspects. One is that of the work itself, its content, or the decision itself; the other is that of the boundaries, constraints, context, within which the work is done or the decision is made. This second aspect is always affected by two determinants—the resources (that make the work feasible, or the decision meaningful) and the objectives.

There are two ways to get work done, or decisions made. One is the direct way, by doing the work, or by making the decision. The other is the indirect but basically equally effective way, by determining the boundaries of the work or of the decision, leaving the actual doing of the work or making the decision to others.

The distinction between these two ways is obvious in an organizational context; the second is *management*, the first is *doing it oneself*. It is not suggested that managers should never 'do it themselves', but it should be recognized by them in this instance that they are not managing, and that this state of affairs needs to be justified. The distinction is a basic one however since the consequences (for accountability for example) are different.

Another feature of the culture in an organization or the style of an individual manager that has sharp structural implications may be described as *distortion*. Decisions tend to be based on a distorted view of what is valuable, what is important, what is needed, and, particularly in large organizations, these distortions can easily become locked-in so that they act as very consistent and damaging constraints on freedom of action. They then begin to conflict with or take over from the explicit or appropriate structure of accountabilities and authority. Improvement in effectiveness requires such distortion to be counteracted, and the starting point for this is an understanding of the sources of distortion. Three frequent sources are:—

Confusion between what is urgent and what is important. Urgent tasks are given priority over important ones. This may be appropriate up to a point, but eventually the 'borrowing of resources' (especially time) from the important tasks prejudices their performance. A version of this occurs when a new highly specific task is allocated into a situation of existing tasks, and because of its newness and definition the task is accentuated more than is requisite.

Inadequate interaction between specific tasks and general responsibilities. A bias due to different levels of definition often occurs; the specific tasks are relatively highly defined and the general responsibilities may be only broadly felt or recognized.

Inadequate weight given to what can only be judged or felt compared with what can be measured or quantified, or at least stated in quantitative terms.

Each of these sources of distortion may be reinforced by the form of policies that operate in the organization (for example, appraisal and payment policies based on quantified results may bias decisions about priorities) and by the style of higher management (for example pressure or enthusiasm linked with tasks personally allocated by the higher manager may bias attention towards the urgent and away from the important).

Furthermore, each of these sources may reinforce each other;

what is urgent is often specified more sharply and more quantitatively than what is important, or general, or felt necessary.

One major aspect of style is that of how the performance of people in the organization is evaluated. The basic point to recognize is that the question of evaluating performance of individuals or groups must be related to the question of evaluating the performance of the organization—its success or failure.

There are many factors, both internal and external to the organization, that may affect the success of an enterprise or of part of one. One internal factor is the inherent performance of the individuals involved, but it cannot be the sole determinant of success since there are always other factors involved, other resources used. It may or may not be the prime determinant of success, depending on the relative weight of the different factors in the particular situation.

Although organizational success depends on many factors, individual performance depends on one factor alone—the capacity of the individual in that particular situation. The enterprise however stands or falls on the basis of its success—or failure. Thus what is of prime importance to the enterprise is not the same as what the individual in general desires to be recognized—his or her inherent performance. In this difference lies the basic cause of some well-known problems in organizations.

It follows that success or failure—that is, results—can never be a totally satisfactory criterion of performance of individuals. People however are ambivalent about this—it is desired that performance should be recognized objectively, that is by the results it leads to, and yet 'results' are rejected as the criterion of performance. 'Management by results' of course is an attempt to bridge this difference, by achieving in the individual an agreement as to the results he or she could reasonably be expected to produce, and thus allowing performance to be assessed accordingly. Since success is never due entirely to individual performance, then performance cannot be entirely objectively identified and measured, but ultimately only assessed or judged.

The individual desires his or her performance to be recognized, not least because it is the manifestation of individual capacity; it is one way in which the individual identifies himself to himself and to others. In paid employment work then considerations of pay and attitude to pay also are affected. The extent to which success/failure is felt to be a satisfactory or unacceptable criterion of performance is likely to be affected by cultural factors, by the implications of failure, perhaps by the timescale of the work, certainly by the kind of work involved.

The role of 'manager' comes into sharp focus in this. The manager is the bridge between the performance of his subordinates and the results they achieve. He can properly only *assess* their individual performance, in the light of the results they achieve but taking into account all the other factors that have affected or even determined those results. This is why the allocation of resources is such an important element of a manager's own work—resources are the basic determinant of results, and given ideal resources for the whole time-span of the work then results *would* demonstrate the performance of the individual in that situation, because the only other factor affecting results would be the way in which the individual used those ideal resources. This is an academic case however, and real situations are more or less distant from this, to the extent that resources are not ideal, do change during the time-span of the work, are affected by external factors, work does unfold or change during its progress, and so on.

Participation

Participation is an aspect of organizational culture, and a topical and important one today, in all fields of organization. There are two main reasons for this. One is that as social culture develops, the notion that most people in organizations are passive resources is increasingly rejected; people want to play an active part in the designs for their future. The other is that as general education improves and the possession of knowledge, skill, capacity becomes more widely spread, active participation is a necessity if these possessions are to be fully and effectively used. In short, participation is both needed and desired, and is closely linked with organizational effectiveness.

It is essential however to realize that the issue of participation is not a simple one—there are various kinds of participation, and their implications for organization design are different. The easiest way to understand the differences is to recognize that participation is to do with work if it is to be meaningful; it is more than 'human relations' or 'being democratic and reasonable'. It is to do with the decision-process, and an understanding of the different elements of that process is essential if questions as to the extent to which people can participate, should participate or should be encouraged to participate are to be answered, in given circumstances, and if organizational processes are to be adequately designed in this respect.

We have already analysed the total decision-process in terms of analysis, decision-making and implementation. These three broad elements of the total process offer different possibilities. Look at them in turn.

Analysis. Sometimes decisions are made on the basis of individual intuition, or even randomly, in the absence of recognition of what data and knowledge are available. Intuition is valuable if it is based on a real feel for the situation, but if other people have knowledge, information or perceptions that are pertinent to the decision then their communication of such information is needed if the decision is to be effective. Decisions should be made on the basis of an adequate analysis of the situation. Unless the person or body formulating the decision has access to all the available data and knowledge therefore, participation by those others that have this access is a necessary feature in this element of the decision-process.

Decision-making. This is obviously a vital part of the whole process. If all the necessary information were available in an appropriate form, there would be no need for a decision but only the application of logic or mathematics. Decisions are needed when there is inadequacy of data, and thus decisions always involve assessment, judgment, uncertainty and risk. A decision cannot be right or wrong, but only more or less appropriate and effective in the circumstances.

The objective of any decision involves implementation of some kind. Even a decision 'not to make a decision', that is, not to act, needs implementation. Thus the potential problems and features of the implementation stage are part of the data relevant to the taking of the decision. In other words, making decisions without regard to their implementation is not likely to be effective. In some organizational situations only one person may have the role and ability to take the decision, but it is always helpful if those who will be involved in the *implementation* of a decision can join or participate in some way in the development of that decision. There can be difficulties in developing decisions however where people from more than one level in an organization participate; these difficulties can be particularly acute if one participant is the manager of the others, where the manager represents certain determinants or constraints coming into the situation from a higher level, and also has certain accountability and authority which are at a different level from those of the other participants. These other participants may resent these constraints or disagree with them, or try to require the decision-taking to be a matter of pure consensus, and sometimes find it difficult to accept that the manager really is encouraging participation.

Another potential difficulty here is that those who will be involved in the implementation of a decision are not necessarily the only appropriate participants; others, who supply information or experience about the situation that requires the decisions may also be appropriate participants. These two sets of participants may have very different points of view, and may even develop into competing groups, one perhaps resenting the other. This can only be dealt with effectively if it is properly understood by all involved, and in practice it is worth considering whether there should be two different kinds of participation, one to analyse the situation, involving all with a contribution to make, and the other to develop the decision, involving only those who will implement it.

Whether or not the basic style of decision-making is participative, the actual process of developing and taking a decision is not a simple one. In most cases, the process is a kind of 'shaping'; a decision is proposed, commented on, modified, argued about—shaped in fact, and eventually crystallized and formulated. The initiative that first suggests a possible decision, however wide of the final mark this may be, usually comes from an individual and not a group. The real group decision is that of agreeing, modifying or rejecting the initiative; it is likely to be one of sanctioning initiatives rather than straight decision-making.

This has a considerable bearing on the form of participation that is effective. An extremely close group culture can inhibit the individual from using the initiative that leads to the proposals for decisions to which the group can respond or react.

The basic issue is that participation is not likely to be appropriate in developing the initiatives, rather the reverse in fact, whereas participation is the appropriate style for achieving sanction.

The end point of the decision-making element is the stating of the decision that has been reached. This is often not recognized as important, but in an organizational situation where accountability and authority are involved it is essential that the decision, when taken, is then *stated with authority*, even if the decision has been arrived at by a process of consensus, or full participation. This *imprimatur* is sometimes felt to be a denial of participation, and it seems more difficult to understand the need for it in a participative situation, but without it the implementation of the decision, in an organizational context, cannot be effective. Where increased participation in decision-making is desired, it is very helpful to discuss and achieve recognition of this point about stating the decision, for it is one that does *not* involve participation but a recognition of individual role.

Implementation. Effective implementation is *always* a matter of individual role and differentiation between what one person does and what another does. Clarity of role is thus the *sine qua non*, and requisite 'participation' in this element has a clear meaning; it is a matter of understanding one's role and 'participating' in it—filling it adequately and with a sense of responsibility. This involves the individual in the role at least sanctioning the organization's authority to determine or approve that role.

Thus participation appears to have different forms and properties, depending on which element of the decision-process is examined. In the analytical element participation is necessary to the extent that required information is gained in this way. In the development and taking of the decision, participation by those who will be affected by the subsequent implementation is helpful because it assists motivation, and it may be necessary in order to achieve a broader-based decision. What this participation should really amount to however needs to be thought out. In the stating of the decision, participation is not a feature. Finally, in the implementation, participation is essential, but it is of a different kind. It is participation in role, and this means in the role/personal relationship with one's manager, and with one's subordinate if one is also a manager oneself.

The implications for managerial style, in a participative culture, are that the manager above all must genuinely accept real participation in the decision-making process. He must distinguish between participation and consultation, and in situations where participation is not possible (for example, where there are constraints or determinants in the situation which do not emanate from those directly involved) or where only consultation is possible, this must be made clear.

The manager should encourage 'participation' in the analysis stage, and recognize the link between this and participation in decision-making. He should realize that decisions must be stated, as well as taken, and that there may be problems of stating decisions clearly in a participative culture.

The manager finally should understand that decision-implementation has different features and different requirements from decision-making.

In short, the manager should be prepared to accept real participation but separate those situations and those elements of the decision process where participation is not possible or not appropriate from those where it is.

A participative situation however puts additional burdens on the participants as well as on the managers. In a simple unit, which involves a manager and a number of subordinates, there are two basic levels of decisions—decisions at unit level and decisions at individual level—and there are three sets of decisions in this context:—

decisions about the unit as a whole;
decisions about the allocation of tasks to individuals;
decisions within tasks, to do with carrying them out.

Decisions in the first and second sets are requisitely taken at unit level and in a manager/subordinate situation this means by the manager. Decisions in the third set are requisitely taken within the framework of decisions in the first set.

One of the arguments for participation is that people should not be put into a position where decisions which affect them are made arbitrarily, without their knowledge. If this is applied, then decisions in the second set should be made as a result of participation between the authority at unit level and the individual. In order to do this effectively however, decisions in the first set must also be made in the same way. This requires the management of the unit (in the sense of the authority at unit level) to be a participatory situation involving all the individuals in the unit.

The focus of attention of individuals however is likely to be their own tasks, at least as much as the tasks of the unit as a whole. Where there is participation in decisions of the second set, at unit level, the focus of attention is still the tasks at individual level. If, however, participation is extended to decisions in the first set also (which is requisite if participation is to be fully effective), then the participants at individual level must be able to act from two different points of view, and two different levels of responsibility—that of their own tasks, and that of the tasks of the unit.

It appears in practice that this dual focus is often very difficult to achieve, and the need puts a considerable strain on individuals at times. A responsible attitude to this dual responsibility on the part of subordinates in a participative situation is vital if the unit, and the participation within it, is to be effective.

In summary, participation is an issue of increasing interest, but it is essential to recognize that there are many facets of participation, for their implications are different. Participation may be necessary for technological reasons, or be forced for cultural reasons. Furthermore, the real organizational situation in the decision sense is not one of decision-making, but of gathering information, taking decisions, and implementing decisions, in simple terms. Each of these elements of the total decision process is different from the others, and needs to be organized in some way. Each may involve participation, but the relationships, the form of participation, the structure of organization for each of them may be different—in the same general organizational setting, and with the same people. A great deal of damage has been done in some well-meaning institutions by a failure to recognize the complexity of participation. A consequence of this understanding is the recognition that a real organization is not a single-cultural situation, but one of multiple culture, style and structure, in which the individual elements may conflict with each other.

Meetings within organizations

An aspect of organizations is meetings, and meetings to the extent that they are planned or designed have a relationship with the organization design.

Meetings are a problem at times for most people involved in organizations. Even if they run smoothly, which is not always the case, they sometimes feel a waste of time, and sometimes what happens subsequently is not in line with what was intended or agreed in the end of the meeting itself. Should a meeting be held when planned, whether or not there is anything significant to meet about? Should there always be an agenda? Should all the members of a meeting be expected to attend, whether or not there are items to be discussed that concern them? Can a meeting make decisions, and if it does, what is the subsequent responsibility carried? These are all questions, amongst others, that are raised frequently.

To deal with these problems, it is helpful to recognize two basic features of meetings. One is that a meeting is a meeting of people; it occurs in a complex set of relationships, affected by what has happened in the past as well as by the situation and requirements of the present and the expectations of the future. It is further complicated by the relationships between the organizational roles occupied by the people in the meeting.

The second feature is that the 'meeting' in the physical sense may contain more than one 'meeting' in the organizational sense. For example, a manager and subordinates meeting together may begin by discussing a technological or professional problem, and at this stage the meeting is one between people who are primarily concerned as having technological or professional expertise. At a certain point however, the manager begins to make decisions about operations, and in this stage the meeting becomes one between people primarily in their organizational roles of manager and subordinates. The manager may then begin to issue instructions to his subordinates, and at this point the meeting may change to one in which subordinates in fact are agreeing on his authority to do so and perhaps negotiating with him the conditions under which they are willing to carry out those instructions. These are appropriate and logical stages of development in a meeting, but they need to be understood if confusion and waste of time are to be avoided.

What do these basic features imply? The first emphasises that we are not likely to understand or deal with the problems of meetings if we regard them as independent and isolated incidents. We need to see them as incidents in a general pattern of relationships through time, often changing, affected by many issues other than those in the meeting itself as well as by those specifically to do with the meeting. The second means that we should not regard a meeting necessarily as a singular situation, but try to understand it as a developing process in itself, recognizing the various stages of this development and their role implications.

A meeting, like any other organizational situation, involves a set of relationships, between roles and between people. It should never be assumed that because a meeting is a single 'geographical situation' it is necessarily a single 'organizational situation'; for an effective meeting the roles and relationships, and how they change, should be recognized by everyone, at the same time.

If meetings are looked at from the decision-making point of view, these seem to be three basic types:—

> those in which decisions are finally taken or really authorized by one particular person;
> those in which decisions are taken or authorized by the majority of the meeting;

those in which decisions are taken or authorized only by unanimous consent of those in the meeting.

Each type is appropriate in certain circumstances. If one person is accountable for the result of the decision (as is the case in the hierarchical manager/subordinates situation for example) then the meeting is of the first type, whatever the type or tone of discussion. The second type is the classic committee constitution, and it is usually observed that the minority accedes to the majority decision after it has been made, or, if this decision is intolerable, the minority resigns. Unless they resign, they are responsible for the decision as if they had voted for it.

A committee constitution is inappropriate where the members of the meeting each have significant power in the situation. Colleagues whose work interacts are often in this position, and failing unanimous agreement they must have recourse to their joint manager. In the extreme form, this may be seen as a situation of negotiation, since a decision that is intolerable to any member, however much that member is in the minority in this, cannot be pushed through effectively if that member has significant power. In the limit, the real situation is that each member of the meeting can veto the decision. A particular case of this kind is where a manager has subordinates whose skills or professional knowledge are vital resources, and ones that the manager does not possess himself or herself. Meetings in this situation are of the third type.

If a meeting is to be concerned with decision-making, then it is essential that the difference between decision-making and decision-implementation be understood. A meeting of any kind is not an effective means of decision-implementing, however effective it is at decision-making; implementation requires differentiation of a role and individual responsibility. There is a connection of course, since the acceptability of a decision to those who will implement it is often as vital as the quality of the decision *per se*, and if those who will implement it have participated in the making of the decision, then its acceptability to them is likely to be enhanced. It is a sad thing to observe however that sometimes participation in the form of a meeting to make the decision has its effect destroyed because there is a lack of understanding that the process of implementation requires a different form of relationships, participation of a different kind.

Research in group psychology has shown that 'member-centred' meetings, in which the leader's or chairman's function is to enable

I

the creativity of the members to be released and to encourage the group's own evaluation of its proposed decisions can be very effect-ive, provided the members of the meeting then understand the need for individual responsibility in carrying out their tasks, whether self-appointed or managerially allocated.

One danger in meetings between a manager and subordinates is that they can become the 'lazy manager's method of co-ordination'. This is not necessarily an indication of fault in the manager con-cerned; the manager may be forced into the situation by the way in which his or her manager manages, or by the general operational style in the organization. An effective manager looks ahead and defines policies that indicate the normal relationships between the different functions and people under him. In other words, normal co-ordination is achieved through the medium of policies. Con-tingencies that are reasonably predictable are also dealt with in this way. The result is that only those incidents or eventualities that have not been catered for require meetings to be held in order that efforts to deal with them may be co-ordinated.

The 'lazy manager' however achieves all or most of the co-ordinating by meetings, either because he does not look ahead and establish policies to deal with all issues save the exceptional, or because his manager co-ordinates his efforts through meetings, so that he can never look ahead adequately, or because either the style of management or the reality of work in the organization is one of 'fire-fighting' rather than 'fire-prevention'. This results in subordinates feeling that most of the important issues are dealt with in meetings, that insufficient preparatory work has been done, and that a lot of time is wasted though there seems to be no other way of getting the information they need about what is going on. The manager however may appear (at least to himself) to be the virtuously indispensable finger on the pulse of everything that is going on—the co-ordinator who is seen by everyone to be doing the job. This is a highly ineffective form of behaviour to sink into, and it can cause consequential problems of damaging magnitude.

II.5 Organizational change

Organization design usually means design for change; it implies re-organization, and re-organization means change in the structure or pattern of roles and relationships in the organization, or part of it, and in the policies and procedures that affect them, to meet new needs, new work requirements, new strategies. This means changed demands, changed pressures on the people in the situation, those people who in reality in their work and their relationships are the effective organization. People are fallible and vulnerable, and in a situation of change need time for discussion and consultation, need support and help, and opportunities for learning and training.

Organizations are really changing all the time, however, whether or not this is reflected in their design, a design change is an attempt to achieve a structure which is more appropriate to the circumstances that exist or are desired in the organization. Sometimes change happens in a way that is not recognized; quite often I meet situations which are structured informally in a way that is not appreciated at all by the people at the top of the organization, yet this informal structure is sensible and effective, and is recognized as such by top management once they become aware of it.

What is often called the re-organization is not re-organization at all, but only the signal for it to begin. Change is a process, not just the definition of a new state of affairs, and the process takes time. Sometimes re-organization fails to be effective because insufficient time is allowed to elapse before the changes are assessed as successful or unsuccessful; further changes are then made and the result is a mess. The effective implementation of a design for change depends on an understanding of the properties of the process, and there are three main things that must be kept in mind if an effective change is to be achieved.

The first, and perhaps the most important, is that of the attitude of mind of those designing the change and implementing it through others. A great deal has been said about the attitude and motivation of those affected by change, but I want to draw attention to the attitude of those involved in affecting the change. The most dangerous state of mind is the tempting one—'Let's get it right, and then get on with some work'. This is a denial of the fallibility of people and of the organization structures and policies they devise. It is essential that those instituting change, at any level, should recognize that it is not possible to get it right. The real process is one of getting it moving, and then reviewing and adjusting the structures and policies as a result of experience. The demands on those instituting change is that *they* shall carry the anxieties of rocognizing that it is not possible to get it right.

The second aspect concerns change itself. In the broad sense there are no discontinuities in the process of change—we cannot jump from one situation to a different one, and it is a cardinal requirement therefore that for effective change in any field there should be a basis of adequate information about the existing situation and its properties. It is essential to recognize this in the field of organization and management, and to ensure that any consideration of the management of change begins with an analysis of the situation that is the starting point for the change process. Even a revolutionary change involves people who have existed and worked in the pre-revolutionary situation; the promise of the new does not detach us from the relationships, the experiences and exigencies, the rewards and penalties in the existing situation. This is the point from which the change will begin, and the movement to the new situation depends as much on its linking with and evolution from the existing situation as it does on the appropriateness of definition of the new situation. Change means weakening existing links in order to build up new ones, and there is always a critical phase therefore in the process of change, when the old links have weakened but the new ones have not yet gained the status borne of the experience of their adequacy. In an effective organization, the structure and policies and procedures enable people to do their work effectively, rather than inhibit them, support them rather than confine them. This enabling effectiveness is what I mean by status, and organizational change is not effective until the new structures and policies have gained such enabling effectiveness—not just clarity, or work-appropriateness, however important these may be. In the interim period support is needed, and an understanding of the inevitability of fallibility (rather than inadequacy) and the willingness to reconsider and adjust.

Earlier, the interaction between the situational structure, the process structure and certain other features such as grading and payment structures was mentioned. If these structures are in conflict with each other, or at best are not adequately related to each other, the problem of change is particularly sharp, for if people are to be supported by their organization, especially when they most need support, then it is essential that those supporting elements are not themselves incompatible. If they are meaningful, they all delineate the areas of freedom of the people in the organization to do their work, to make their own decisions, to use the resources available to them. Too often, certain elements of organization structure, or policy, or procedures, which have not been incompatible in the old situation, cause serious difficulties in the new, not because they have changed, but because their relationship with the new situation is different from that with the old. It is important to develop all those factors which delineate the freedom of people in their work, all the structural factors, so that they enable rather than inhibit, reinforce each other rather than interfere.

The third point is the most obvious. Effective organizational change means the development of effective relationships between people, sometimes new people, and new work, in new settings. If the design problem were to develop better 'designs for work' or better 'designs for people' it would be complex enough. But the real problem is that people and work are different issues, and have different properties. Thus effective organization will always be a compromise, compromise between what is desirable from the work point of view and what is at least tolerable and preferably acceptable to the people doing that work. We should expect to find different compromises therefore; not a uniform kind of structure everywhere, but different structures to suit different circumstances. Do our plans for change allow enough room for compromises, for differences? Do we have the possibility of honest communication between the people involved in change, so that the differences, the compromises, can be explored properly? The need for communication, discussion, consultation, participation, is obvious, and who should be involved should be identified as part of the design for change. One issue that sometimes arises and must be dealt with properly follows from the fact that some elements of change may not still be open to discussion. They may not be within the power or authority of those concerned with the change to alter. It is essential that if this is the case it is recognized honestly. If time is too short, or some of the features of the changes have already been decided at a higher level in the organization for example, this must be disclosed. An almost fatal error in some attempted changes has been that certain determinants or constraints in the situation have not been disclosed until too late.

In any organizational situation there is an interaction between the organizational or work aspects and the personal, and in a situation of significant change, this interaction changes. For example, when a new technology is being introduced, the existing organization structure may for a time (before it is modified to meet the demands of the new technology) become of very little consequence, and the personal aspects become more important, as people learn how to operate the new technology. As the situation becomes more stable however, and the people involved gain confidence in it, the organization structure, if effectively modified, will begin to take on a full meaning once more. In a situation of change, the organizational aspects (the accountability and authority structure) wax and wane in relative importance to the more nebulous (but in these circumstances stronger) elements of power and responsibility as the organization changes and subsequently re-stabilizes itself. A stable organization, facing the need to change, must 'shake itself loose', become more fluid, in order to allow change to occur, but must then re-stabilize itself in order to be effective. If an organization is to remain coherent in the instability phase, when the organizational aspects are weak or irrelevant, then the personal aspects must be strong enough to be the basis of this temporary coherence. When the relationships in the organization have settled down again, the organizational aspects should be re-established in order that they shall be the source of coherence, freeing the personal aspects for their proper role. Sometimes however the strength of the personal aspects inhibits this re-establishment.

Any effective process of analysis of organizational situations leads to the recognition that change occurs in three main aspects, whether change is inherent or deliberately contrived. These are the aspects of the work itself, the people involved, and the environment within which the organization exists and operates. Each of these aspects must be examined and considered, but what in practice is even more important for management than an understanding of these aspects and their dynamics is an understanding of their interactions and the implications (some of which are conflicting) of their relationships. This understanding in turn gives a manager an understanding of what can and what cannot be done in terms of managing change—what the range of organizational possibilities is and what the constraints and determinants are that affect the outcome of his decisions about change.

One further point is this. Resistance to change is usually based on a real or potential sense of insecurity, or on the view that the exponents of the change will gain from it, whilst others may well lose. It therefore follows that intellectual argument alone will not surmount these emotional barriers; it may perhaps carry the day in the short run but lead to longer-term resistance, anxiety and conflict. Security and an honest exposure of the gains and losses in a change, for all concerned, must be developed if the change is to be effectively achieved.

II.6 Design in the future

What features of organization design are we likely to see in the future? I think that certain trends are becoming clear already, as a result of more thinking about organization structure and more observation of actual organizations and how they are changing. The past ten or fifteen years have seen a great deal of technological change in organizations, technological in the widest sense. Apart from purely technical changes, such things as mergers, new formations, international groupings and new pressures from the human resource and changes in other resources such as information have all added together to make 'technological change'. But to a great extent the organizational development that is needed to encompass these changes so that their effects have their full benefit has not yet occurred. The next few years are likely to see a considerable amount of this development however, perhaps more than any other kind, and the trends can be seen in many different organizations.

In many instances organizations are becoming more complicated. Their significant environments are becoming more complex and more pressing in their effects. Furthermore, organizations in the future may not be able to gear their main efforts only to one of the environmental features, such as their market, but may need to relate with energy and priority to various features as each becomes for a time the dominant one in terms of its effect on the organization's survival or effectiveness. Many organizations now are meeting problems of increasing size, and the activities going on in them in many cases are tending to increase in complexity and in level. At the same time, as I said earlier, often the demands of the organization have outstripped the reasonable possibility of finding people to meet those demands. I am not talking in a superficial way about people reaching their level of incompetence, but in a deeper sense of the relationship between a person, especially a manager, and his role showing a profile of competence that is not comprehensive. This can demonstrate itself as a concentration on one or two aspects of the work in the role at the expense of others, or a talking about other aspects without effective action. An example is the concentration on short-term or specific objectives at the expense of less definite long-term development, or sometimes the reverse of this—the escape from present reality into the future. I am sure that we have reached the stage in some situations where the organizational form will have to be changed, away from what is theoretically desirable, in order to enable human managers, with their limitations, to be respectively competent, relatively effective, in their roles.

I think there is no doubt that the properties of what I have called the 'process of work' will increasingly become the main determinant of organization design, and the main focus for policies and procedures, styles of management and leadership. This has the implication that a 'multiple role', 'multiple relationship', 'multiple style' organization will develop as the normal one; groups will form and re-form as the different tasks require or the processes of work change, and relationships and styles will vary, depending on what part of the whole process of work is involved, or which of the environmental features is the dominant one at the time. At the same time, the dilemmas in real organizations presented by those factors connected with change and flexibility on the one hand and stability and coherence on the other will be faced more effectively. The result is likely to be an increase in the development of the matrix type structures already mentioned—project or task structures based on specific task requirements, with an underlying structure concerned with the human aspects of stability, career, longer term relationships and the general survival features of the organization.

Another way of putting this is that the successful organization in the future will be the one for whom change is the normality, not the occasional perturbation, yet which can achieve the stability and coherence that is essential for survival. Change will be designed for; the structure will be geared to change; it will be a process structure. What is left of the situational structure however will become more meaningful, not less, because it will be the framework for the stability and coherence needed.

The skill, knowledge and creativity of people is likely to be needed more and more as the most vital resource in any organization. A feature of a process structure is that competence in the

K

work becomes the basis of the status of people in the process, and competence is a matter of relevant skill, knowledge and creativity. This kind of resource demands involvement and participation; it has power to challenge the way organizations are structured and people managed. Thus the process-structured form of organization is both encouraging to the greater recognition of the importance of the 'knowledge resource' and increasingly insisted on by that resource.

People in organizations are changing. The level of education is increasing, and the content of education is changing. More participation will be needed, and demanded. Particular problems will increase, of a kind that is familiar to us in certain situations already, where the technical demands of the work require highly intelligent people to deal with them and yet the work must be very closely controlled. Job enlargement and participation, encouragement to development thinking, as a means of giving adequate work-satisfaction in such situations will have to be taken very seriously indeed. More people perhaps will behave as if they were self-employed, moving from project to project, or organization to organization as work-interest attracts. (I believe that much of this is going on today, though it is not apparent; the movement of people from firm to firm in industry for example seems to be increasing sharply in some countries, and the sense of 'making a career in the one firm' is dying away.)

In many cases, people in organizations are becoming more aware of the organization's environment; they are developing views about what the organization's relationship with the significant environmental features should be like, and about what features should be regarded as significant. People outside the organization are also developing views of this nature, and the result is bound to be that organizations will have to be structured increasingly to enable more environmental features to be related with effectively and dynamically. The simple idea of operational tasks related to one significant feature such as market or clients will probably become inadequate, and all this leads to a further reinforcement of the trend towards process structure and a matrix kind of organization design.

The task of management will increasingly become one of 'setting the stage', since the work-process itself will determine the 'direction of the play'. Management will explicitly become an enabling process rather than a directive one, and it will need to be understood that just as room must be left for the subordinate's reasonable freedom of action in the way managers manage their subordinates, so the same freedom must be recognized when their work is process-controlled.

This shift of managerial task from the direct management of work to the less direct management of the setting or context of work requires the manager to encourage motivation of the subordinate by leadership, sometimes of a self-effacing form, with the subordinate effectively managing his own work.

Curiously enough as management becomes less direct and organizations more democratic in the sense that managerial authority is no longer regarded as a right to be used arbitrarily, even if wisely, the need to question the use of authority may not become less. In any social system, however decisions are made, their implementation always involves differentiation of account-ability and authority. Even when decisions have been made in a truly democratic or egalitarian way, their implementation is clearly in itself not 'democratic'. Wherever authority is positioned, whether in the roles of Boards of Management, or committees, or individuals, its exercise is unilateral. Whether this exercise of authority has the desired effect however depends on the reaction of those over whom it is exercised. Herein lies another element of the concept of democracy—that the use of authority should be properly sanctioned. Now sanctioning is a matter of consensus, or, in a society with universal franchise, the majority vote. To achieve this sanctioning in an effective way, it is necessary to develop consensus so that it reflects general and real awareness of issues, and not just the noise of a vociferous few against the background of a passively uninvolved majority. This development must involve the questioning of decisions, focusing of attention on the use of authority, trying to ensure that issues are properly understood and faced, insisting on elucidation of information, and so on. This kind of probing and shaping of con-sensus may appear undemocratic because it takes a minority to do it, but in fact it is a vital part of the democratic process and is seen to be such once the relationship between sanction and effective authority is understood.

Warren Bennis, in his paper 'The Coming Death of Bureaucracy',* spelled out some of these issues very clearly. He used the term 'bureaucracy' to refer to what he called the 'useful social invention that was perfected during the industrial revolution to organize and direct the activities of a business firm'. He went on to suggest that

* *Harvard Business Review*, 1967.

most students of organizations would say that its anatomy consisted of the following components:—

A well-defined chain of command.
A system of procedures and rules for dealing with all contingencies relating to work activities.
A division of labour based on specialization.
Promotion and selection based on technical competence.
Impersonality in human relations.

and he described it in general as 'the pyramid arrangement we see on most organization charts'.

He identifies at least four relevant threats to bureaucracy:—

Rapid and unexpected change.
Growth in size where the volume of an organization's traditional activities is not enough to sustain growth. (A number of factors are included here, among them: bureaucratic overheads; tighter controls and impersonality due to bureaucratic sprawls; outmoded rules and organizational structures).
Complexity of modern technology where integration between activities and persons of very diverse, highly specialized competence is required.
A basically psychological threat springing from a change in managerial behaviour.

He goes on to say that the organizations which survive will be those which cope with these threats adequately. He suggests that 'the tasks of the organization will be more technical, complicated and unprogrammed. They will rely on intellect instead of muscle. And they will be too complicated for one person to comprehend, to say nothing of control. Essentially, they will call for the collaboration of specialists in a project or a team-form of organization.

The social structure of organizations of the future will have some unique characteristics. The key word will be temporary. There will be adaptive, rapidly changing temporary systems. These will be task forces organized around problems to be solved by groups of relative strangers with diverse professional skills. The group will be arranged on an organic rather than mechanical model; they will evolve in response to a problem rather than to programmed role expectations.'

These are Warren Bennis's views, but I think they can be paraphrased as 'organizations will become more process-structured and less situational-structured, and the values regarded as relevant in them will become more the "process" values of competence and knowledge and less the "situational" values of status, position and right'.

Similarly, Drucker* has recently been saying the same kind of things, in a different way perhaps. He has suggested that a new view of management's role is needed, in terms of:—

management being both a 'science' and a 'humanity';
management's task being to enable knowledge to be more productive;
management's accountability, even in business firms, for 'quality of life' as well as 'profits';
management's need to encourage entrepreneurial innovation.

Again, I think these views can be paraphrased as 'management will become more aware of the balance needed between the organizational and the human aspects, will recognize human capacity as the resource that really matters in the long run and will understand the importance of capacity objectives as well as output objectives'.

One thing the future is likely to hold for some organizations is a limit to further growth, where growth means expansion. It seems however that organizations must either grow or stagnate, and therefore expansion will have to be replaced by other forms of 'growth'. Organizations will continue to grow, but expansion, or extensive growth, will be replaced by intensive growth—internal improvements, better use of resources, better quality of output perhaps; in short, growth will be in effectiveness rather than in size.

For most organizations there is the possibility of both kinds of growth. In a limited market, an industrial firm may grow by increasing its share of the market, but also by using its resources more effectively so that its share of the market grows in profitability. Some firms have discovered that growth of the first kind does not automatically lead to increased profit; I sometimes have the experience of being told with due pride by a managing director about the growth of his firm in terms of turnover, market share, short-term profit, and then to hear from others that the trends of costs, quality, profitability, are in the wrong direction. Growth in size is being achieved at the expense of effectiveness. A proper

* *Harvard Business Review*, 1969.

balance must be achieved between these two kinds of growth, and in the future the externally-determined limits of expansion may mean that the major field for growth is in effectiveness.

Intensive growth can only be achieved by better organization and more effective management. Extensive growth often happens as a result of luck, market changes, technological developments, but unless it is followed up by intensive growth then problems are bound to occur and viability is bound to be threatened. There are several well-known examples of this.

Intensive growth inevitably is the result of better organization and management, whereas extensive growth may or may not be.

There is an attitude factor here also. We tend to feel that extensive growth is real growth, and a change is needed so that we value intensive growth as much.

Decision-making itself is likely to change, not fundamentally but in terms of techniques and information flow, and the effect will be to require a re-distribution of the real decision-making in the organization structure, and a re-distribution and probably re-direction of the human decision-makers. It may be that the basic human decisions will become 'policy' decisions or 'political' decisions, weightings and value judgments, which are then processed along with the facts by what are described as 'decision-making techniques' in order to lead to the decision.

One effect of the style in organizations becoming more participative, less autocratic or authoritarian, is that knowledge about the operations and activities going on in the organization is shared by a greater number of people. A result of this is that the minor inadequacies and inconsequentialities, the small stupidities and nonsenses that are present to some extent in all organizations become exposed to those working in the organization, and questioned and criticized; in the past they have remained unchallenged because they were not perceived so clearly. If managers are to remain credible in the eyes of their subordinates, and subordinates' motivation is not to be damaged, these problems, which in the past could be ignored, must now be dealt with. They will tend to be problems of detail, since the illumination that exposes them comes largely from below.

At the same time, it is slowly being recognized that the damage done to the organization by the small inadequacies, when added together, may be greater than the effect of what appear to be much larger issues. This point may be felt more strongly by those not at the top of organizations.

On these two counts therefore, it appears that in the future senior management will need to concern itself with improving those aspects of the operation that appear small in comparison with the big issues of business strategy, new policies, new technologies, as well as with the big issues. Many of these small aspects are to do with implementation of the big decisions, and draw attention to the inadequacy of understanding in many organizations of the factors that enable effective decision-implementing to be achieved.

One example of the kind of thing that may happen in the future occurred in a seminar on industrial organization in 1968 for young European graduate managers. A consensus developed the view that 'we contest the nature of the consumer society', and a reflection of this view was a challenging of what were felt to be the basic objectives of their organizations. It may be a very significant feature of organizations in the future that this kind of challenge may come not only from people outside the organization who are opposed in some way to it, but by high-capacity individuals inside the organization who are likely to become senior managers.

At the same time it should be recognized that if an organization is to remain viable by design rather than by accident, its structure, policies, priorities, operations, style must evolve to meet the pressures on it, and the perceptions, knowledge, assumptions and decisions on which those organizational features are based must be recognized and examined continually, consciously and critically. They must be challenged.

The ability to challenge is present in the organization if its staff are well trained (as contrasted with 'brain-washed'), but it needs to be channelled if it is to be effective. The channelling itself however must not be so arranged or institutionalized that the challenge becomes muted, or only allowed if it is 'constructive', for it should always be kept in mind that if challenge is to be effective it must at times be destructive to some extent. Management training, particularly of the analytical kind, can greatly help an intelligent manager who is genuinely trying to understand the organizational and personal behaviour he observes in his work. It can and should allow and encourage discussion about the appropriateness of such behaviour. A question sometimes asked however is whether an organization can afford analysis of its own behaviour, or whether such introspection can disturb and disillusion some individuals who without it would go on with their work in blissful ignorance of the real issues. Reality suggests the opposite—that an organization cannot afford not to engage in such introspection and challenge if it is to be effective. Much evidence indicates that as the complexity of operations in organizations increases, so does the need for managers to develop a realistic understanding of the organization and how they relate with it, and to interpret and communicate this relationship to their subordinates. Einstein said 'It is nothing short of a miracle that modern methods of instruction have not yet entirely strangled the holy spirit of curiosity'. It is possible that some management training may quench this spirit of enquiry and challenge (the spirit may be a distressing phenomenon for top management perhaps, who may describe it as 'rocking the boat'); the organization of the future must not make this mistake.

There remains the question of stability and fluidity. If either the organization itself or its relationship with its environment is too stable or too fluid, then risk to viability arises. On the one hand, the risk comes from inertia, on the other from incoherence. What will have to be aimed at in the future consciously is a situation in which there is an effective partnership between change and stability. The prerequisites for this are knowledge and confidence. Without confidence, stability degenerates into inertia, preventing flexibility and change rather than acting as a springboard for them. Without knowledge, perceptions of change and its implications are distorted, confidence is affected adversely, and thus again flexibility and change are inhibited. The organization of the future will need to pay much more attention therefore to the development of knowledge and confidence in its members.

Finally, I think more organizations will find the need for a focal point of thinking and review within themselves, an 'internal consultant'. All too often, changes achieved deteriorate because no group exists within the organization to maintain and modify where necessary the new structure or new operations. Whether this role of internal consultant is filled by an individual or a group, a certain knowledge and attitude of mind will be required in it, and it will be an *internal* role; the job cannot be done by an external consultant, because the issue will need to be faced continuously. The external consultant should be involved to bring in new ideas and to act as a point of reference outside the organization. The essential quality of the internal consultant is that he should be capable of understanding that there are no right answers to the questions about organization structure, especially when innovation is needed, and should be able to deal with this kind of situation, the situation of dilemma. In detail, this means essentially that the internal consultant should be analytical in approach, should perceive the conflicting factors, the dilemmas, that this analytical approach exposes, and should be strong enough to establish working solutions to those dilemmas, and even stronger, to review and change those working solutions when they in their turn become inadequate. These working solutions, I emphasize, need strength in both the proposer and the implementer, because they mediate between conflicting issues, conflicting pressures, whose strengths are often increasing in a modern efficient organization; they are not the result of bad organization, but of good organization.

General bibliography and further readings

Part I

Exploration in Management (Brown, Heinemann 1960, Pelican 1968).
Organization Analysis (Newman and Rowbottom, Heinemann 1968).
Rules, Roles and Relations (Emmet, Macmillan 1966).
New Patterns of Management (Likert, McGraw-Hill 1967).
Structure and Process in Modern Societies (Parsons, The Free Press 1960).
Planning and Control Systems (Anthony, Harvard 1965).
Systems of Organization (Miller and Rice, Tavistock 1967).
The Social Psychology of Organizations (Katz and Kahn, Wiley 1966).
Organizations (March and Simon, Wiley 1958).
Administrative Organization (Pfiffner and Sherwood, Prentice-Hill 1960).
The Enterprise and its Environment (Rice, Tavistock 1963).
The Rational Manager (Kepner and Tregoe, McGraw-Hill 1965).

Part II

Company Organization—Theory and Practice (Barnes *et al*, George Allen and Unwin 1970).
Changing Organizations (Bennis, McGraw-Hill 1966).
The Management of Innovation (Burns and Stalker, Tavistock 1961).
Organizational Analysis—A Sociological View (Perrow, Tavistock 1970).
The Motivation to Work (Hertzberg *et al*, Wiley 1960).
Motivation and Personality (Maslow, Harper and Row 1970).
The Professional Manager (McGregor, McGraw-Hill 1967).
Industrial Organization (Woodward, Oxford University Press 1965).
Organizational Psychology (Schein, Prentice-Hall 1965).
The Reality of Management (Stewart, Heinemann 1963, Pan Books 1967).
The Planning of Change (Bennis *et al*, Holt International 1970).
New Perspectives in Organization Research (Cooper *et al*, Wiley 1964).
The Practice of Management (Drucker, Heinemann 1955).

Glossary

Certain terms are used in a more specific way than usual in this book, and it may be helpful to bring them together in a Glossary. The problem is not just one of semantics, but of concepts; if the concepts that are being used can be clarified, then agreement as to the terms employed to stand for those concepts is made easier. This Glossary gives the main concepts used in this book, at their present state of description, together with the terms used for them here. These are not the right terms, nor the wrong terms; rather they are the selected terms, for the purpose of communication. The descriptions of the concepts are not exhaustive definitions, but minimal descriptions to enable the concepts to be identified and discussed.

Accountability, the relationship between the person or group and their work-activities that is organizationally determined; the organizational requirement for activities to be carried out.

Activity, the physical and mental actions that link the availability of resources with some kind of outcome.

Authority, the access to resources that is organizationally determined; the relationship between the person or group and their resources that is organizationally determined.

Capacity objective, the objective to do with continuing ability to meet other objectives, at a given level.

Chief executive role, the role in which there is accountability for the activities of the executive system as a whole.

Collateral relationship, the relationship between roles whose work interacts directly where neither role involves authority over the other.

Cross-over role, a role linked by authority with lower-level roles whose work interacts.

Decision-process, the process of deciding what to do and then doing it; the process includes analysis, development and taking of the decision, and implementation.

Enabling resource, a resource that enables working resources to be obtained or changed or their use affected.

Executive system, the set of roles in an organization, through whose occupants the work of the organization is carried out.

Managerial role, a role in which there is accountability for more than that which the occupant of the role can or will accomplish single-handed.

Objective, an achievement or goal that is aimed at, desired or required to be met.

Objective of directionality, a statement of objective that indicates the direction in which action is required, an open-ended statement.

Objective of intention, a statement of objective that is so general that it does not give a rational basis for deciding tasks.

Objective of result, a statement of objective that indicates the standard of result desired, a closed statement.

Operational tasks, those tasks that follow directly from output objectives.

Organization structure, the various parts of the organization and how they relate with each other.
　　Process structure, the structure of the processes of work, in particular the decision-process, in the organization or part of it.
　　Situational structure, the structure of positions and functions, or roles, in the organization or part of it.

Output objective, the objective to do with what the organization or work is for, at a given level.

Personal objective, the factors made up of the objectives, needs and expectations of the person that affect the relationship between the person and his work objectives.

Power, the personal link with resources; the ability and willingness to use them.

Relationship analysis, the identification of basic features in any relationship, in terms of the entities involved and the content and process of the transactions between them.

Resources, the various elements that are needed to be available and used in some kind of combination in order to carry out activities.

Responsibility, the personal way of carrying out activities.

Role, the set of expectations placed by the organization on the person who occupies it; the statement of role must include some indication of objectives, activities and resources.

Sanctioning system, the system of roles and relationships to do with the power of individuals and groups interacting with authority in the organization in which they occupy work-roles.

Situational structure, the structure of positions and functions in the organization, or part of it.

Task, a piece of work that is closed or bounded in terms of objective, resources and activities.

Work, the situation of resources, activities and objectives; the process of using resources to carry out activities towards objectives.

Working resource, the set of resources used directly in all work, involving time, material and human resource.

Index

(G denotes item in Glossary)